Tough As Nails: Finding Your Voice as a Woman in the Workplace

With 10 Strategies for

Overcoming Mean-Girl Cultures,

Myths about Job Loss,

Negotiating Tips,

and Much More

Joanne Rencher

Frayer & Williams Publishing
P.O. Box 16
Florida, New York, 10921

Frayer & Williams Publishing books are available: at special discounts for bulk purchases, for sales promotions, for educational or corporate use. For more information, contact the Author at JoanneRencher.com

Library of Congress Control Number: 2018913655
ISBN: 978-0-9763464-2-5

The content provided herein does not take the place of legal advice from your attorney. The Author has made every effort to ensure the accuracy of the information within this book was correct at the time of publication. The Author does not assume and hereby disclaims any liability to any party for any loss, damage, or disruption caused by errors or omissions, whether such errors or omissions result from accident, negligence, or any other cause.

There is no content in this book which has been included for the purpose of disparaging, or otherwise highlighting any particular organization or person known to the Author. Every example, circumstance or personal vignette in this book has been pulled from the Author's decades of living and working. Any resemblances to real organizations or persons the reader may know is purely coincidental.

Dedicated to my daughter, Kiara ('Kiki')

By God's grace you will soon be entering the marketplace—full of energy, knowledge and a desire to make a lasting difference in this world. I pray that this book will arm you with the tools, insights and understanding needed to be, and do, all that has been destined for you, my love.

CONTENTS

10

Acknowledgements

The seeds of this book were planted many years ago. Those seeds have now produced fruit, divinely used for a purpose far greater than my own personal and professional plans. I'm grateful that I eventually ran out of excuses, and was left with that unmistakable calling to complete this. Writing this book has been incredibly hard work, but an absolute labor of love. As a first-generation American, I owe my parents, who came to this country with so little—absolutely everything. While my heart aches to know that they will never read this as they have both passed away, I am buoyed by the knowledge that their precious 'deposits' in my life are an indelible part of these pages. Their wisdom, grit, nurturing and love are part of who I am—and who I am still becoming. Advancing this book through each stage, until I could eventually see the finish line could never have been possible without the support, encouragement, coaching, coaxing and love of others in my life. I'm grateful for the colleagues and friends across the years who suggested that I use my God-given gifts to author a book. Many people spoke words of encouragement into my heart which I would later draw from. In recent months, there were three ladies who gave of themselves in ways that I deeply appreciate. Greta Cowan, Nancy Karas and Karen Robilotta read the earlier versions of my manuscript in the midst of their own busy lives and careers. Each comment, edit, and thoughtfully communicated piece of feedback, made a wonderful difference in the final product. While running their own businesses, tending to a sick child or flying across the country—they gave generously of their time and energies. As I write this, I'm thinking of our three children, Marcus, Malcolm and Kiki. Each of them inspires me every day to make my own deposits into their precious lives, to help them along their journey. I couldn't be prouder of each of them. And, I've left the very best for last—my husband, Steve. When God brought us together more than three decades ago, I received the gifts of a soulmate, best friend, and the love of my life. He has been the wind beneath my wings, reminding me who I was created to be whenever life's challenges dampened my spirit. From start to finish, my husband used his incredible intellect to lead me through the entire process of publishing this book—down to every detail. There are no words beautiful or eloquent enough, to express what he means to me. It is my privilege to be his wife.

Introduction

When I first began writing this book, I thought that it would be mainly an encapsulation of my career—a career shaped over more than 25 years in the profit and nonprofit sectors, and within both the domestic and global arenas. However, I soon realized that it would be *so much more.*

The first part of the book's title—*Tough As Nails*—is meant to convey just that: toughness. It is also meant to ascribe that toughness to the collective sisterhood all over the globe. So, if that part of the title also makes you think of beautifully polished fingernails on a woman, I'm perfectly fine with that!

But, how exactly does a woman develop this toughness? Toughness is fueled by strategically building a diversity of skills and tools over the course of your career. However, even with all of these skills and tools, I can virtually guarantee that you will be ineffective without the power and clarity of your own voice. It took me many years to find mine.

I grew from an extreme introvert to one whose passion is now helping others to find their own voices.

Your voice can make a difference—if you develop an astute understanding of *how*, *when* and *where* to use it. The difference you make will impact not only your own life, but the lives of every person with whom you come into contact.

I do realize that those reading this book will be at varying stages of your lives and careers. My heart's desire is to lovingly challenge you, at whatever stage you're in.

For some, you may be sliding from day to day, week to week, month to month—in misery. Perhaps earlier in your career, you believed that you might be able to positively impact your company, and the business world at large. As the years progressed, you found yourself periodically stuck. You are no longer clear as to how to use your natural talents, nor how to effectively develop new skills. Along your career journey, you may have become increasingly confused as to how to leverage the support of influential others who can help you. Or worse, you may be battling through toxic workplace cultures with ineffective leadership, mean-girl behavior and/or the paralysis of broken processes within your company. As a result, your Sunday evenings, previously devoted to restful times with family and friends, have now become moments of dread as you brace yourself for the return of a new workweek.

For others, you are aspiring or more seasoned leaders, and everything in between. Regardless of where you are along this leadership spectrum, you have one thing in common with your sisters: you are looking for a fresh path. You have either just begun to realize the need for newer and healthier habits, and the competitive advantage of sharpening your skills—or you have simply made the decision that <u>today</u> is the day to do just that. I applaud you.

For yet others among you, life has dealt you an unexpected blow. You have been catapulted onto a new road—a crossroad. The choices which you'll need to make will have tremendous implications for you and your family. They may also contain hidden gems of opportunities and one *heck'uva* personal reinvention story—a story which you may decide to pen someday. I take that journey with you, and endeavor to guide you through the fogginess of such a period—and into your purpose.

And, if you're looking to simply get to know yourself better, to understand what makes you tick and why—or to help others develop that awareness, this book is also for you.

The book is written in such a way that you can read it sequentially from start to finish, or grab a specific section that may speak more specifically to you, and begin to dig in there.

Each Chapter ends with 'Big Ideas' that help you to capture, and remember, the major takeaways. At the very end of those Chapters, I also share 'pearls' from my life journal which give you a window in to what makes me tick.

Tough As Nails: Finding Your Voice as a Woman in the Workplace is chock-full of tangible tools, practical advice, insights and guidance for how to be your *authentically awesome* self.

#BecauseYouAreWorthIt

Now, get going...there's no more time to waste!

With much love and a spirit of encouragement,

Jo

Chapter 1

Your Special Sauce

The workplace can be a tough environment. You'll have to be even tougher.

A tough-as-nails mentality is needed to successfully navigate any number of challenging scenarios which serve as distractions and impediments to effectively performing your job. Developing the skill to cut through the noises which too often block the sound of productivity, is both an art and a science.

A big part of that navigation is awakening to the realities of office politics. I personally like to call 'balls and strikes' and dislike gamesmanship in the workplace. But, office politics exists in every corner, cubicle, and bathroom of a workplace. It's best to accept that fact and learn how to use your talents in any setting, without compromising your values. There are additional ingredients required for a tough mentality: high doses of resiliency, creativity, and when life dictates, the ability to reinvent yourself. I'll share some of my own vignettes of self-discovery and reinvention later on.

Those who differ in some way from what conventional wisdom suggests are the more common, high potential, promotable leaders, will have additional hills to climb.

Women entering the workforce in particular, are up against an array of stereotypes that box us in and can thwart our ascension into more senior ranks. The irony is that the business world, without more women, is robbed of the diversity of thought and perspective which we bring to business tables. The numbers confirming this void, while driven by myriad factors— are still staggering.

According to the Center for American Progress[1], though women earn almost 60% of undergraduate degrees, 60% of all master's degrees, 47% of law degrees and 48% percent of medical degrees, and are 47% of the U.S. labor force—they still lag behind men in their representation in leadership positions: They are just 25% of executive and senior managers, 9.5% of top earners and 6% of CEOs in S&P 500 companies.

While gender bias, discrimination and nagging stereotypes are all very real issues, there exists a huge opportunity for women to take better control of their futures by exercising more introspection. The result of such introspection should be an acute sense of self-awareness.

We each have specific beliefs, motivations, behaviors and traits which are part of our true essence when we show up to the workplace. So, who are you?

What are you doing when you are the most, or least confident? When is the last time you did something—personally or professionally—that is completely new? Would someone who doesn't know you be more likely to describe you as confident or cautious? Do you know what your top three strengths and weaknesses are?

Unless you truly know yourself, you'll be far more susceptible to the whims and behaviors of others. Knowing yourself is akin to having a read on your physical self. When it's cold, you know it and can then make the necessary adjustment based on the external environment. You can choose to dress warmer, or, depending upon the length of time exposed to that environment, you can tough it out. In other words, you alone know how much you can take.

In one of my podcast interviews recorded for my website (wgninhr.org), I spoke with Richard Goeglein, Chairman of the Executive Committee and Director at Volunteers in Medicine, Southern Nevada. In that interview, entitled, *Leader Know Thyself*, he talked about the importance of knowing what you really want as a professional. He then encouraged my listeners to toss their hats into the ring and to pursue the thing that excites them. As Richard shared, there are a host of personal assessments available to help you peel away that very delicate onion called 'self.' One of them is the VIA Personal Characteristic assessment survey.[2] Another one of these assessments is the DISC Personality Test.[3] DISC will give you greater perspective on what drives you the most and how you're likely to behave in a particular environment. Gaining clarity on what makes you tick is key to engaging effectively with the rest of the world. This self-awareness is what I describe as the equivalent of looking into the mirror to observe the obvious view, then swirling around to help you, and others, fully understand what you look like from several other angles.

Hold Your Ground

There are more than a few ways that a woman can, unwittingly, relinquish the essence of who she really is. Workplace dynamics can sometimes collude with our own bad habits to result in that dreaded state of hovering beneath one's potential.

This means that you may need to unlearn some bad habits. That adjustment will enable you to show up better prepared for the many 'environmental' challenges found in the workplace.

How many times have you witnessed a woman allowing herself to be cutoff during a meeting when she has not yet made her point? Perhaps, you may have even been the perpetrator. And, I've seen far too many women in meetings who begin to verbalize a thought or idea, only to have someone else—who was certainly not the resident mind reader—jump in prematurely to correct them.

Why being interrupted or corrected is proven to happen more often to women (even by other women), is fascinating, and a study unto itself. Business and thought leaders tackle this topic with regularity.

According to Jessica Bennett's January 14, 2015 Time article, there are far too many "manterruptions" (men interrupting women) or "bro-priations" (ideas raised by women which a man refines and takes as his own). But, Bennett also writes that women may "pitch an idea, perhaps too uncertainly—only to have a dude repeat it with authority. We may possess the skill, but he has the right vocal cords—which means we shut up, losing our confidence (or worse, the credit for the work)."

Bennett's assessment is curious. Losing your confidence and relinquishing the credit for your work to someone else, is not an acceptable response to being interrupted or having your idea stolen. Becoming meek during the settings which Bennett describes, should never be due to fear of the bad habits of others—or because of their "vocal cords." All of us fully own our behavior and must make the necessary adjustments if that behavior is working against us.

In fact, we actually lose some of the strength in arguments which rightly take issue with "manterruptions," until and unless we honestly and courageously conquer our own self-defeating tendencies. This requires pushing back against the behavior of others. We can no longer simply talk and write about it—we have to be accountable for doing it.

Getting sentences out is a personal triumph of mine. As a child, I spent my formative years in virtual silence. I was an introvert's introvert. I struggled with everything from my body image to the gap in my front teeth—and everything else I conjured up to magnify what I viewed to be imperfections. Days were filled with self-doubt, and nights were filled with self-loathing. As for school, while parent-teachers conferences were full of positive reports on my grades, there were more than a few furrowed brows among teachers who openly opined about how quiet I was. I was convinced that they viewed me as an anomaly.

As I left those years and entered young adulthood, I eventually found my voice in the world. Finding my voice in the world, led to finding my *leadership* voice in the workplace, as I'll share in greater detail later on. And, as a learned extrovert, I've also discovered the joys of motivational speaking. These opportunities allow me to encourage others, which has always been a deep passion of mine. Now, it's tough to get me to shut up when I have a full head of steam on a topic of great interest or importance to me.

So, being interrupted or corrected is something that I'm personally sensitive to, having worked so hard to be heard. Every circumstance holds the potential for me to use my voice for what I hope will be to someone else's benefit. My current day philosophies have deep roots in my childhood experiences, and my discoveries have been central to reaching the top of my field.

Now, I use my leadership voice with great excitement as an executive leader. I remember being in a meeting years ago where someone was doing a post-mortem on a pilot program which was launched months earlier. I looked at the document which the presenter provided and was about to quote some of their statistics as I positioned my question. No sooner than I could reference those stats—which were already clearly in writing—did two other people jump in to correct me. They hadn't the foggiest idea of what my question was. What's worse is that they almost derailed a vital learning opportunity which later surfaced as a result of my question. I was forced to stop (twice!), look at the culprits, and let them know they were interrupting me. I then continued with what was, ultimately, quite a productive discussion.

Women must do more of the 'leaning in' that is all the rage these days. The not-so-earth-shattering response to self-defeating or sabotaging behavior is found in Nike's advertising brand statement, *Just Do It*. Take the reins, and be tougher in order to create new realities.

It's vital that the essence of who you are never be stifled. At times, that means fighting for the air time in meetings, finishing the point you were making even when others seem impatient, and never letting yourself be corrected when you're clear about the concept being discussed. In the latter circumstance, you can always acknowledge another point of view, or even change your own—but only *after* you've effectively expressed yourself.

This may require seeking some coaching on how to project your voice with confidence, or displaying the type of body language that exudes decisiveness and authority. It also means having (or digging deep for) the confidence to stand your ground when needed. Not doing any of this is a choice. If you choose not to, is there any wonder why a man within your corporate circle may be better positioned to pounce on opportunities to shine—even when he may not even have the best grasp of the subject matter? In Chapter 3, I share more about getting out of our own way as women in the workplace.

Navigating New Environments

Aside from the self-inflicted wounds which negatively impact a woman's leadership presence, there are other factors which will test our leadership mettle. Beginning a new job with the responsibility of managing a team with members who are significantly older and more experienced, is one such factor. Another, is being asked to take on a role outside of your own area of expertise. Each of these situations requires skillful navigation.

It's quite natural for a new job to bring high degrees of performance anxiety and a persistent sense of having to prove oneself. If you've inherited a team as a woman, and are now leading people who happen to be significantly older and more experienced, you are undoubtedly faced with a daunting task.

Roughly ten years from now, more than half of the global workforce will be comprised of Millennials. The generation preceding Millennials—Generation X—is currently aging beyond their prime working years. Among the newest generation—Generation Z—will be those who have entered their prime years in the workplace. They will soon be working alongside their older Millennial predecessors.

These generational workers will all be part of a dynamic workplace whose workers are tackling increasingly complex and thorny business issues, and doing so from different parts of the globe. It is not hard to imagine that my Generation Z daughter will find herself, in her first real job out of college, managing a 60-year-old man. She, and other women like her, will need an arsenal of tools to operate effectively and credibly.

Women leading increasingly diverse teams will also need to be adept at assembling them to work in the digital age with extreme agility and creativity. These types of teams will naturally result in complications, even beyond the age disparities.

For you to be successful as a leader in these settings, you must develop the skill to lead with authority *and* influence.

It won't be enough for you to be outgoing and personable. If you are responsible for managing people twice your age, you will need courageous leadership. You must be able to take risks in your approach and decisions, share unpopular perspectives and lead with confidence—particularly with team members who may not have the most confidence in you at the early stages of your tenure.

And, while women are generally seen as the gender which is better able to demonstrate empathy, empathy without emotional intelligence is limiting. Leaders with high emotional intelligence are adept at managing their emotions. They understand their personal triggers and know how to adjust when external circumstances may be challenging. You must be able to parlay empathy into the skill of understanding what motivates and discourages other people as you lead these diverse and dynamic teams. When conflicts arise, you will need to demonstrate the ability to do what I've described for years as 'stepping into it.' Stepping into it means making the conscious choice to directly address an issue which is clearly uncomfortable, or previously seen as off-limits.

Avoid a Common Plague
One of the more common pitfalls in the workplace, for any leader, is what I call the plague of groupthink. I believe that

women have to be particularly aware of succumbing to this. The uniqueness of your voice should never be stamped out by an inability to distinguish your own original thoughts and opinions from the crowd.

Groupthink, according to the renowned research psychologist, Irving Janis, occurs when people set aside their own personal beliefs to adopt the opinion of the rest of the group. Janis completed the most influential work on this topic, gleaning from case studies like the Bay of Pigs debacle, and Pearl Harbor. While you may not be dealing with plans to equip a guerilla army to push a nation's leader from power, you will be dealing daily with a fair degree of hostility to new ideas and approaches in the workplace.

One of the symptoms of groupthink, according to Janis, is self-censorship; muting one's opinions for fear of being ridiculed or ostracized. Fear of being ridiculed or excluded from the inner circle, is one that stems from the earliest days of childhood experiences. And, research on gender differences in learning tells us that girls tend to be more self-critical and prone to feelings of failure from very early on.[4] Even when performing at or above average, girls are often far more focused on pleasing and will internalize disappointments, believing that they have not lived up to expectations. The dark side of these struggles can manifest itself in mean-girl behavior, which has an ugly, grown-up version in the workplace. I have devoted an entire section of this book—Chapter 4—to dissecting that dark side.

In a workplace dependent upon a freshness of approaches, bold thinking and risk-taking, we can ill-afford to suffer paralyzing flashbacks from our youth—where a desire for perfection can result in the delay of the next disruptive innovation!

With all the work, conversations, and best practices on the topic of diversity, in the final analysis, you are different because you hold unique interpretations of the world. You see the world and circumstances through your carefully crafted lenses and experiences.

While societal influences, and individual personalities play a major role in shaping how you show up in the workplace, the natural differences between the sexes are evidenced both anecdotally and scientifically. As a woman, you will pick up cues around not only what's being said, but *how* it's being said. Research at the Indiana University School of Medicine suggests that men listen differently than women.[5] The study demonstrated that women may appear to use both sides of the brain, while men listen with a focus on the left side of the brain. The right side is believed by scientists to process more non-auditory functions. According to that study, none of this was thought to have an ultimate impact on performance, only that language 'processing' is different between the sexes.

This means that you will enter the equation in different ways, which should be equally celebrated and intentionally sought. Holding a divergent opinion in an otherwise unified set of perspectives, is tough. In fact, it's tough to be different, period. Have you ever experienced being the only one not to know something or someone in a group? Or, how about that time when you had a thought which made perfect sense in your mind, only to express it and have the entire room look at you as if you had two heads?

We need all voices at these business tables—and that includes your unique *female* voice. Business problems are becoming increasingly complicated, requiring creative solutions. To not speak up and out, in spite of the barriers—self-imposed or not—is to rob your colleagues of your brainpower.

The sea of sameness is boring. It's too easy. It lacks creativity. If you're aspiring to the top, that ascension requires a key ingredient—you. Companies will need all of you in order to get to their next level of greatness. You represent their competitive advantage.

Tough As Nails · Big Ideas

✓ Knowing yourself makes you less susceptible to someone else's idea of what you have to offer

✓ Don't live up to the worst stereotypes of female behavior. Create new realities

✓ Holding your ground and taking your rightful credit is a choice...make it

✓ Acquire more tools to increase your effectiveness in managing diverse and dispersed teams

✓ Your independent thinking is a win-win...an ability to think differently will be part of your company's competitive advantage

Pearls from Jo's Journal

I've never been satisfied with the mundane. Routines always bored me senseless. I've learned that change brings with it enormous opportunities—opportunities to learn, to grow and to go to new levels both personally and professionally. Even changing my pocketbook regularly is a great way to refresh my thinking and approach! On a practical level, a change of pocketbooks forces me to focus on what I really need, what I prefer and what I can do without. Beyond that, the change actually puts me in a different mood—bold, chic, casual, etc. We need variety in life to stay dynamic. William Cowper, the British poet said that "Variety's the very spice of life, that gives it all its flavor." Variety in our lives is a great enabler to finding our own 'special sauce.' Once we do, our jobs are then to acquire more life lessons and tools which help to refine us...to make us better. That's how we can grow into the best version of ourselves.

Chapter 2

Be the Sharpest Nail in Your Company's Chest

I f I asked you who within your company is considered a leader, would you recite the names at the top of the organizational chart? I hope not. *Everyone* is a leader. And, as such, every leader should be striving to increase their individual value—to be the sharpest nail in the company's chest.

You have a wonderful opportunity to bring your own brand of leadership to an organization, using your distinct voice to advance the mission and strategies. This signals that you have a genuine concern for the enterprise to which you belong. The best leaders have their pulse on the broader issues of the larger organization—revenue challenges, customer perceptions, staff morale, the launch of new programs, etc.

You bring a set of unique skills, talents and experience to your position. Provided that the position is fulfilling and the right match for your background, you need to be shrewd in regularly reminding your employer how much of a gift you are to them. As women, we tend to be less inclined to tout our value and vocalize our talents. However, your shyness, false humility, or fear will only ensure that people will be struggling to remember your last name as opposed to singing your praises.

Table Stakes

First, ensure that you're meeting the basic expectations of your job. While it's true that most companies wrestle with accurate and up-to-date job descriptions, there's never a legitimate excuse to remain unclear about the core responsibilities for which you were hired. If unclear, you should engage your manager in a productive conversation. Don't outsource this responsibility to human resources—it's up to you and your manager to ensure that your job description is up-to-date and accurate. When you initiate the conversation with your manager, be constructive to avoid turning it into a complaint session. Once clear on those basic expectations, don't look to simply score—go after homeruns. Offer suggestions and insights on ways to increase your value, even beyond the minimum job expectations.

Put yourself in your employer's shoes. They need demonstrable evidence that you have the tools that can help them get to new levels. You can prove this by increasing your value through your performance. Then, any requests for increased compensation will be more likely to be viewed as reasonable and justifiable. Asking for gender pay parity when your performance is not on par with your male counterpart sets the entire cause back decades.

Pull the Right Levers

Develop an acute understanding of the key business levers for your company and look for ways to pull them. Beyond the unique business levers for your company which enable product or program advancement, and increased revenue, there are even more obvious levers to pull. Effective management of expenses is a great place to add value. Here are a few thought-starters for you as you uncover the many opportunities to do this at your own company.

- Understanding the cost-revenue structure as part of expense management is vital. But, it's only the first step. Many companies may struggle to manage costs without ever assessing the dynamic relationship between those costs and the revenue being produced. This assessment may reveal ways to increase the return on investments through smarter or less spending.

- Inefficient business processes are a severe drain on any business. Cumbersome work flows, redundancies, lack of clarity on who has decision-making authority and gaps in processes, are all culprits which suck the life out of businesses daily. It shouldn't be too difficult to spot them in your company.

- Small changes can result in significant savings. For example, reviewing your supplier invoices, vendor contracts, and any wasteful company practices are easy places to start.

The more you know about your business, the more you can position yourself to positively impact it.

Get Creative

Recognize the importance of innovations which can emanate from your corner of the workplace. Oftentimes, we think of innovations as the creation of the next Post-It Note. Not necessarily. Innovations can stem from the smallest idea or simply a shift in thinking. If you're the closest person to the delivery of your company's key product, you have the unique ability to see what's working and what isn't. Innovation can also come from the unlikeliest of sources. At the Massachusetts Department of Correction, one of the guards suggested a change in the way that the Massachusetts Department of Correction stored their inmate photos. Rather than take pictures with film and store them, the innovative idea was to use digital cameras and a database for image storing. This suggestion was purported to save the Facility over $50,000 in just the first year of implementation.

There are countless other stories of people in the world who, upon observing a nagging issue, used their imaginations to take action. From bendable straws to pop tops on soda cans, relative unknowns stepped into their self-made laboratories to change the world. Why not you?

Negotiating for More Money

Once you're operating as the sharpest nail in the chest, opportunities to negotiate your value—in dollars and cents—will present themselves.

So much has been written about the difficulty women have in asking for a salary increase or negotiating job offers. I do believe that we struggle with a host of issues as we work up the nerve to expect, then ask for, more. Working in the human resources field, I've seen firsthand how many women seem to have a higher tolerance for taking a back seat, working harder for less, or settling for being that go-to resource who never gets the credit. Call it virtuous, or a generous heart—but it has its limitations. Given my experience on both sides of the negotiation table, it's clear that poor negotiation skills among women contribute to broader pay disparities. However, I view the issue of pay inequity as far more complex. One must consider much more than equal pay for equal work. Factors such as: the number of women who decide to apply for particular jobs; legitimate selection criteria leading to women being hired into jobs traditionally held by men; and individual competencies, must all be considered in assessing reasons for earnings and pay disparities. However, my focus here is on a woman's ability to negotiate with confidence, clarity, and to be tough as nails while doing so. Here's what I've learned to help you negotiate better—whether in red stilettos or Oxford wingtips. (However, I'm more so talking to the stiletto wearers among us.)

- There is an opportunity cost associated with choosing not to negotiate, nor ask for a raise when the time may be right. Those decisions, calculated over several years, result in a lesser income and reduced benefits associated with that income. Thinking in those terms may motivate you to operate differently.

- Be mindful of the broader context and your ability to influence the situation during negotiations. If the prospective job is in a small company and based in an area with a significantly lower cost-of-living than your current location, a tougher negotiating approach may reflect poorly on you. Instead, employ some creativity by asking for other perks to be included in the offer package.

- Cancel every thought you have about rejection during negotiations—i.e., *They'll see me as greedy or self-interested; I'll suffer the pain of rejection; They won't like me as much.* The stories you play over and over again in your head will always be far grizzlier than the realities of those interactions. The worst-case scenario of not getting that pay increase, or having to walk away from a great job that was simply priced too low, should never be a soul-crushing occurrence. Move on. Building that negotiating muscle will make it easier to use.

• Practice your negotiation skills when the stakes aren't as high. It's much easier to haggle with the person selling costume jewelry at a county fair, than it is to negotiate a starting salary at a new company. When the stakes are low, you can practice your ability to push back, test the limits of your negotiating counterpart and where—and when—you draw the line to walk away from the negotiating table. Assess your comfort level as you pleasantly decline the price offered. Have a quiet debriefing session with yourself to rate your success in negotiating, and determine what you might do differently next time.

• Align around the company's needs and your value. Take the time to understand the actions required from the role and the desired results being sought. Then, identify precisely what you bring to the table in terms of your own talents so that you can describe your value in terms that will resonate. This allows you to approach negotiations with a true win-win disposition. Be sure that you've thought well in advance about your 'blue-sky' salary number, as well as the number below which you would never accept. This clarity will help you to avoid moving any goalposts that you may later regret.

- Clarity comes from doing your homework. Research the heck out of the topic being negotiated. I personally like to be overprepared—for just about every situation. I'm the type of person who will look for reams of data, articles, and even tangentially related facts on a subject as part of my research. I may be a bit obsessive, but it increases my confidence level tenfold, and helps me to shift gears more fluidly during negotiating conversations—because I have that much more data to work with. This applies to *every* type of negotiation. As it relates to salary negotiations, sites like Glassdoor and Payscale can help you to understand yours, and the job's market value.

- During the negotiations, ask questions which help you to remove the layers of information which could be masking the core issue—i.e., is the first salary offer you received more about internal equity on the team, or is it a budget issue? Is there a willingness on the part of a new employer to revisit compensation in six months, after mutually agreed upon goals are met?

- Never use your current salary or salary history as the starting point of your negotiations for an external job offer. You now have some legislation backing you in this area. In efforts to address pay inequities, several cities and states in the U.S. are—or will be—banning employers from asking about a candidate's salary history.[6] This places your skills and talents at the heart of salary negotiations.

- Your expenses and personal budget issues, are not your employer's problem. There should not be even a hint of those motivations in your negotiation discussions.

- Work hard to put yourself in the position of having job alternatives. Your negotiating power is greatly increased by having alternatives which, in turn, give you the option of walking away should negotiations fail. Walking away at the end of a job search process is certainly not to be taken lightly, as both you and the prospective employer will have already expended precious time and resources. However, walking away is a demonstration of your value. The employer's response will let you know whether they're in agreement with that value assessment.

Other Ways to Increase Your Value

Here are three additional cups of wisdom which I've returned to drink from many times in order to do my own gut-check, or when coaching others through crucial conversations.

Know which role along the career path you're most interested in pursuing. If you don't do well with extreme pressure, you shouldn't be pursuing C-Suite roles. If you'd rather manage numbers and data rather than people and personalities, that team director role is not the best choice for you.

Keep good records. I'm a diligent notetaker and try to stay organized around my email trails as well. This is not about covering my rear (though that does come in handy). Good records will help to keep you on track, focused, and they can clarify any confusion around work or projects which directly impact you. This habit demonstrates your diligence to others up, down, and across the hierarchy. While it may seem like a small thing, I can assure you, it really makes a difference.

Be your loudest champion. I've often heard people say things like, "my work will speak for itself." That may be true, but the sound decibel is louder when *you* are the one who is doing the speaking. Remaining quiet while your fantastic work is being gleefully described without attribution is folly.

Become more comfortable with claiming your work. Find creative ways to describe the outcome, what it took to make it happen and what impact it has, or will have, on the company.

It's true that there's no 'i' in team but there's an 'e' for effort—so, claim your own efforts and champion the results.

Tough As Nails · Big Ideas

✓ Before you expect to be appreciated as the sharpest nail in your company's tool chest, be sure that you're doing the basics of your job

✓ Operate in your own self-made laboratory to find innovative solutions to nagging problems

✓ Build your negotiation skills by practicing in lower-stakes situations

✓ View negotiating as a right-of-passage needed to increase the value of your gift

✓ Master the art of negotiating to increase your success in asking for more money, or accepting the right job offer (pgs. 18-22)

✓ *To thine own self be true.* Don't put your hat in the ring for roles which you know are not for you

✓ Be your loudest champion

Pearls from Jo's Journal

Just as the contents of a gift remain unknown until it is unwrapped, so too can our own gifts remain hidden to others until we take more initiative. Over the years, I've learned the importance of understanding every nook and cranny about the business which I'm a part of. I make it a point to become close to not only the financials, but to the finance colleagues who manage them. I also like to understand what other functional leaders are worried or excited about. Not everyone will appreciate your gift or your initiative, however. I once had a (female) boss actually laugh out loud as I shared a slide deck of what I believed to be very innovative ideas for a new organizational design—including a recommendation for my promotion in the new design. It was a bold move, but certainly not outrageous nor inappropriate given the dire state of the company at the time. Sadly, while I received no input on the content which I'd spent an entire weekend working on, I was forced to sit through a 10-minute lecture on the need to pay my dues. At the time, I was far enough along in my career to cause that dues-paying lecture to fall flat. This reminds me of one of my favorite quotes from Ted Rubin, Leading Social Media Strategist, Keynote Speaker and Brand Evangelist: "Your value does not decrease based on someone else's inability to see your worth."

Chapter 3

Unblock Your Own Path to Being
Authentically Awesome

Let's start with a newsflash: men and women are different! There are biological differences between us. When a woman gives birth, she can't share the joys of breastfeeding with a man. And, generally speaking, if you need to move a large piece of furniture across the room, you're likely to look for a man to do it. Why? Because men have a higher percentage of muscle mass than women in both their upper and lower body.

In our fight for gender equality and women's rights, too many women are fighting for men and women to be the same. The former is honorable, but I believe the latter to be a bridge too far. Differences exist and women should embrace them—and without fear of being called a traitor to someone else's feminist ideals.

As our XY chromosome-brothers 'evolve' within the workplace to make room for the diversity of thought and backgrounds entering, we are presented with yet another opportunity. It's an opportunity to be what I love to describe as *authentically awesome*. For me, that description covers the gamut—from leadership styles to lipstick colors (more on lipsticks, later)!

The first step toward recovery from the fallacy of homogeneity in every aspect, is admitting that women simply operate differently. However, there are some differences which can often work against us as women. We must learn to better hone certain leadership skills. I believe that we can accomplish that even while retaining the parts of our individuality which preserve our authenticity. Staying true to ourselves is not incompatible with challenging ourselves to be better leaders. In other words, we must take care to not become part of our own problem.

Sorry, Not Sorry

In the past few years, I've made a concerted effort to dramatically reduce the number of my apologies in business settings. I've taken a microscope to myself to find that I was apologizing in excess, and often completely unnecessarily. Meeting conflicts, inadvertent scheduling mishaps, innocent misunderstandings, and the like, should not be responded to with apologies.

I certainly was not alone. Women, in general, too often apologize for virtually every occurrence known to humankind, and maybe even those known to canines and felines for that matter. *Sorry, were you sitting there? Sorry, what's the correct spelling of your name? Sorry, can I have another plate without the piece of hair in it?*

Politeness has its place in the workplace and cordial behavior is always the preferred approach as we interact with each other.

However, excessive apologies demonstrate weakness and uncertainty—two traits which are typically not attributed to the best leaders in the workplace. And, yet, the fact that we tend to invite these descriptions through our penchant for apologizing, somehow, seems lost on us. It will always be hard to convince me that describing an overly apologetic woman as lacking in self-confidence is tantamount to gender bias. This behavior among women gives validity to those most dreaded of stereotypes.

Beyond the apology syndrome, surprisingly, is oftentimes a child's voice in a woman's body. Uptalk—where declarative sentences end with awkward-sounding, rising inflections—is a female leader's worst nightmare. I've attended many meetings where an impeccably-attired, credentialed woman opens her mouth to uptalk, and instantly loses credibility. It's bad enough that it conveys a lack of confidence, but it also sounds ridiculous. We should lovingly correct our daughters, sisters, friends and yes, even the female leaders among us who express themselves in this way. We owe it to each other to point this out.

I know of an organization, ironically one with a strong coaching and development philosophy, where I'm told that most of the female population practices uptalk—as if members of a strange club. It's not clear whether they joined with this bad habit, or simply adopted that speech pattern as part of their way of assimilating.

It should go without saying that women leaders can't afford to sound unsure of ourselves. Our peers and team members depend on us to navigate the waters, make tough decisions and provide direction—even when we're not certain of the outcomes. Uptalk is an enemy to all of those leadership actions. There are a few things you can do to attack it.

First, become intentional—starting right now—about listening to yourself talk. Become more self-aware. Are you guilty of uptalk...even a little? If you are, then practice (in the privacy of your bedroom or shower, please) making declarative sentences. I heard someone suggest that reading the preamble of the Declaration of Independence is a helpful way to combat uptalk. After all, holding a truth to be self-evident leaves little room for questioning. If you're looking to kick the habit of uptalk, you'll need to get to the root causes of it, as it may be a symptom of a deeper problem. Do you resort to uptalk when you're unsure of a particular topic? You are certainly worth taking the time to explore and address what may be at the core of that habit.

The Personal Side of Business

Here's another female tendency: taking business issues personally. I actually believe that taking issues personally is perfectly acceptable. We are complex human beings with an array of emotions, experiences, temperaments and life experiences. When we step into the workplace, we can't simply drop some of our baggage off before we hit the revolving doors. We bring our full selves to work—for better or for worse. This too comprises the essence of who we are.

Not taking business issues personally is no more possible than trying not to smile at a tasteless joke. Even though you know the joke shouldn't be funny, smiling just happens naturally.

That said, women can take personalization to extreme levels. When there is a dicey business issue to hash out, where viewpoints are intensely shared, it is often the woman who will be more focused on someone's feelings. The next day, she will assume that those hours of heated business conversations the day before must mean that there are relationships to be restored with colleagues. Conversely, our XY chromosome-brothers will have typically forgotten about the prior day's exchanges, and will already be onto something new. One explanation for this disparity is that women tend to have a stronger focus on leading with compassion, as reflected in a Pew Research Center Survey.[7] Compassion at work certainly has its place. However, if you're in a leadership position or aspiring towards one, you will need more than compassion to avoid having heated issues derail your effectiveness.

Ultimately, you will need to develop the *art of personalization*: bringing your baggage to work, unpacking it skillfully—and with compassion—yet never becoming weighed down by someone else's baggage.

This is vital, and learning how to do this effectively will save you years of stress and self-induced trauma at work. Over the course of my career, I've had countless difficult conversations with people in the workplace. Each time, I've tried hard to manage those types of interactions by striking a delicate balance: communicating information rationally from the head, while expressing it kindly from the heart. It is a skill which I continually hone.

We are all flawed human beings. In addition, there are individuals within any given workplace who may have been hurt deeply in their lives. Hurt people, hurt other people. So, while developing the art of personalization is necessary, it won't inoculate you from pain which can result from the behavior of a colleague or boss. But, knowing how to handle your own emotions through self-awareness will make you less vulnerable to the behavior of others in the workplace. As I shared in the first chapter, know who you are, and then embrace that knowledge. It will help you to build your backbone, particularly if you're working in an especially tough workplace environment.

A 'Must-Have'

Tendencies towards perfectionism and self-critical behavior are often at the center of a woman's struggles to be decisive. In Chapter 5, I outline 6 leadership traits which I believe are essential to being effective, whether you're an aspiring or a well-seasoned leader. I include decision-making among those traits. I feel quite strongly about the importance of demonstrating decisiveness as a leader. Hence, in this section, I spend more time helping us to understand the many nuances of that particular skill.

Decisiveness is absolutely critical to advancing your business, particularly in complex situations and during these times of such extreme unpredictability. In the May-June 2017 edition of the Harvard Business Review (HBR), authors Botelho,

Powell, Kincaid and Wang compellingly outline what they describe as the four essential behaviors which set successful CEOs apart from the pack. One of those behaviors, is "Deciding with Speed and Conviction." According to the data used in that HBR article, those who made decisions more quickly and with conviction, were *12-times* more likely to be high-performing CEOs.

Decision-making is a skill which I personally prioritize as a leader. I view it much like three legs to a stool, which collectively, comprise what I describe as the importance of *relentless decision-making*: what and where decisions need to be made, the effectiveness of those decisions, and knowing who holds the decision-making power.

As much as we as women desire to build consensus, not everyone needs to be involved in every decision. There are big, high-impact decisions, and smaller, more mundane decisions that must be made every day throughout a company. Each of those decisions should sit at the appropriate level within the company. Otherwise, there will be little distinction made among the time and rigor spent on each of them. There's no time to waste in business—results matter. If a decision-making process requires multiple sign-offs from those sitting at multiple levels, confusion and frustration will abound. It also signals a lack of trust in those assigned to the work. Worse, if the ultimate decision-maker is a woman, those kinds of cumbersome processes may suggest that she does not have the confidence to make, and fully own, the decision. That's never a good look.

I'm sure that you can name at least one decision that resulted in a less than stellar outcome, expended too many team resources, and took entirely too long to make. The ability to make high quality, speedy and efficient decisions in today's business world sets companies apart from their competitors. Some hiring processes are stark examples of the most egregious failings of decision-making in companies today. I've worked across many sectors, domestically and globally, and have borne witness to hiring managers' inability to make decisions about candidates during a search process. In those instances, the hiring process itself, along with hardworking recruiters, are often scapegoated as the problem. In reality, it is the decision-maker who is unable to move towards a clear and timely outcome. Oftentimes, this has cost the particular organization not only time—which equals money—but top talent who ultimately decided to move on to another opportunity midway through the search. Women in charge of the decisions, which I observed over the years, were certainly not the only culprits. However, I can say that they managed to reinforce every female stereotype during those particular hiring processes—excessive analysis, avoidance of conflict during disagreements and penchants for unnecessary consensus-building. Struggling to make a hiring decision after three rounds of candidate interviews, changes to the job description, multiple debrief meetings with the interview panels and an 'interview dinner' with two finalists—is excessive. Bite the bullet and make the decision if you have the power to make it.

Teams with whom I've worked have heard me say repeatedly that, if everyone has the 'D' (decision-making power), no one has the 'D'. It's simply not practical, nor effective, to diffuse decision-making across several parties. Someone must own the ultimate decision and be tasked with soliciting input, synthesizing it, and making a final recommendation. Team decision-making for the sake of consensus-building becomes muddy, and actually increases the chances of conflict. In those scenarios, processes will inevitably drag on with unclear results.

This three-legged stool of relentless decision-making is a non-negotiable skill which every woman needs to sharpen at each stage of her career.

Decisions move businesses forward. Lack of decisions cause dissension, wasted energies, and lost opportunities. In some cases, the consequences of poor decision-making can even cost lives. To fully grasp the enormity of that statement, one need only research the tragedy which resulted from the largest marine oil spill in history. At the root cause of that disaster, was a series of poor and delayed decisions that led to the Gulf of Mexico oil spill in 2010 caused by an explosion on the Deepwater Horizon oil rig.[8] There were early warnings of a problem on the rig which, if heeded, could have avoided the catastrophe. Instead, those in leadership roles became mired in faulty decision-making and political calculations. While these grave situations are obviously not commonplace examples, decisions in the workplace are made daily and the livelihood— if not the lives—of employees depends upon excellence from leaders.

Yes, successes and failures in decision-making are committed by both men and women. However, I am among those who believe that women are not fully convincing the broader population of their prowess in this area.[9] The good news is that we absolutely have the power to change that.

From 'Mad Men' to Equal Opportunity Struggles

It wasn't terribly long ago where men were chasing 'skirts,' engaging in sexual innuendos and unabashed sexual harassment. Women were hard pressed to get ahead without the assumption that they had slept their way to the top. Men were the trumpeted 'breadwinners' and women were the stay-at-home-moms, with the exception of the largely single secretaries generally referred to as 'girls' by their colleagues. During the *Mad Men* era which spanned the 1960's, women were employed in roles thought to be more suitable to their gender—i.e. nurses, secretaries. In the decades to follow, progress was slow but steady as women joined traditionally male-dominated professions. Most people would have to admit that, today, progress is still insufficient. The #MeToo Movement tells us that the days of reckoning and recovering from the more abhorrent behaviors, in and outside the workplace, are not yet firmly behind us. And career choices and advancements which close the gaps in traditionally male dominated professions, still lag behind. For example, there is still a dearth of women working and leading within the STEM industries (science, technology, engineering and math).

The challenges of fighting for more time to be spent on life issues and family needs, is much more of an equal opportunity struggle. Both men and women are desperately seeking flexible work arrangements. Many—not all—employers are finally realizing that the results you produce are far more important to obsess about than the 'where' and 'when' of your work product. As long as it works for the business, the array of programs to help balance work and life—whatever that means to you—are vast and necessary for women, in particular, to achieve professional advancement. Women in leadership increasingly have more champions and supportive programs which aid them in striking a better balance between the urgent and the important activities. However, our ability to skillfully discern between those two categories, is still an ongoing struggle.

What is 'urgent', really? Is it every email that lands in your inbox flagged as high priority? Is it that meeting which a colleague's assistant has persistently invited you to attend? Is it measurable by volume—or is it the 'weight' of the source? Tending to everything keeps women—and all of us—stuck in an unpleasant and suffocating paradigm of responsiveness. Being able to "do it all" is a vaunted arena where few can claim that they visit with any regularity. It's a rather silly place to be. We should no more strive to do it all than we should attempt to juggle fifty plates on our heads knowing that several of them will inevitably crash to the ground.

In his book, *Essentialism: The Disciplined Pursuit of Less*, Greg McKeown writes about the power to choose in order to focus on the most essential activities in one's personal and professional life. McKeown writes that "when we forget our ability to choose, we learn to be helpless. Drip by drip we allow our power to be taken away until we end up becoming a function of other people's choices—or even a function of our own past choices. In turn, we surrender our power to choose."

Stop giving away the power to determine what, and to whom, you give your precious time and energy.

Being—and Staying—Authentically Awesome

By now, you may have noticed that I enjoy using the term *authentically awesome*. While I add a variety of descriptors to it, it actually means whatever it's supposed to mean for you. It reflects your uniqueness—your most authentic self. It tells everyone something about you through the way you carry yourself, your style choices, your way of thinking, speaking, and of being. As long as those descriptors are not harmful, obviously offensive to others, or self-degrading—they are part of what makes you authentically awesome. It's important to resist the pressure to conform to someone else's ideal of what 'awesome' is. This is particularly challenging for women in the workplace as there are reams of literature, guidance, and classes on what to wear, what not to wear, what attire to choose for interviews, etc. Even decisions between open or closed-toe shoes in certain settings have become part of heated debates.

There is an assumption that we will all conform to a prescribed norm, especially as it relates to women. While it's smart to conform to some degree in order to avoid operating as a rebel without a cause, it is equally as smart to retain the essence of what makes you, *you*. I'm sure that you can recall examples of people who made hasty judgments of women in the workplace. Many of us may be guilty of this. Nevertheless, we'll never recognize the importance of our own individuality until we identify those areas in our lives where conforming feels inauthentic.

I wear purple lipstick. Sometimes, the particular shade of my purple lipstick is so pigmented that it can actually look blue. I love my purple lipstick—and the entire rainbow of colors in my makeup chest. This love is not just because the colors stray from the norm, but because they scream something else about me— the fullness of my lips. This is important to me. As a child, I was teased incessantly about my lips. I was regularly made to feel as if I was carrying two balloons beneath my nose. Kids can be cruel. The net effect was that I resorted to biting my lips when I wasn't speaking, eating, drinking or sleeping. That was a ridiculous look, but I believed it to be a necessary part of self-preservation.

I also love clothes and fashion. My colors are often bright, and my choices do not hide what is a generous posterior. This physical feature was also something which I was relentlessly teased about growing up.

I share more about my metamorphosis in the last Chapter, but suffice it to say that, now, I fully embrace all of me. I fought long and hard to finally embrace my authenticity and develop self-confidence. Through my faith in God, caring people, and an amazing husband—I can now say that I'm authentically awesome. So, why would I relinquish my hard-won individuality for the sake of conformity? With the exception of high-impact situations, and political landmines which may have longer-term implications, I believe that it is possible to resist conformity. I've developed my list of non-negotiables regarding my authenticity. What are yours? I encourage you to put a stake in the ground around them. You should also recognize the fact that harsh criticisms and vicious comments are not limited to mean kids. Women are often the worst offenders and can be the architects of behavior that is ultimately harmful to the collective sisterhood. These kinds of shallow critiques chip away at our progress—in the workplace and in society at large.

I shared those personal examples to describe the importance of our individuality, however, there are many others that reveal broader challenges to working women. When Marissa Mayer, former CEO of Yahoo, made the very personal decision to take two weeks of maternity leave following the birth of her twins, the backlash and naked outrage on social media was over the top. Yahoo's parental leave policy is generous, thanks to Mayer's own leadership following her earlier pregnancy. But, that wasn't good enough for the many women who believe that being female requires us to march in lockstep to every cause and opinion affecting our gender. Mayer's response to all of this should have been summed up in six words—*it is none of your business*. Women shouldn't presume to speak for their entire gender any more than a black person should attempt to speak for their entire race.

Being authentically awesome is most fruitful when we: 1) get out of our own way, 2) maximize opportunities to grow, and 3) fight for the right to our own individuality—within the boundaries of the law, common sense and, where applicable, our own religious observations. On the issue of individuality, Robert Louis Stevenson said it best: "To know what you prefer instead of humbly saying Amen to what the world tells you you ought to prefer, is to have kept your soul alive."

Tough As Nails · Big Ideas

✓ Differences between men and women should be celebrated

✓ Hammer away until you spot, and conquer, self-defeating habits

✓ Be compassionate as you personalize issues in the workplace, but don't carry others' baggage

✓ Effective communication requires both the head and the heart, particularly when delivering tough messages

✓ There are certain leadership traits needed to set you apart as a leader...being decisive is *key* among them

✓ You maintain your power when you choose wisely regarding how your time and energy is spent

✓ Identify those areas in your life where conforming feels inauthentic—then put a stake in the ground around them

Pearls from Jo's Journal

There is only one You. A mother can look at her identical twins and still be able to tell them apart. And, those twins' personalities are informed and shaped by their environments and experiences—just like the rest of us. Individualism has its limits, of course. We don't want rogue employees, unruly children, or renegade soldiers. We need order and some degree of conformity. But, I've found that it's so important to embrace your authenticity as part of life's journey—even in the small things. It tells the world who you are. Once, a friend was sharing my picture in my biography with a businessperson. My friend later shared with me that this businessperson commented negatively about the purple lipstick which I was wearing in the picture. They apparently felt that it hurt my chances to be taken seriously as a business leader. If my professional experience, accomplishments and reputation can't speak more loudly than my lipstick, I have far more problems than color choices. And, I would encourage others to work harder to hear and see the more substantive things beyond one's lipstick color.

Chapter 4

Drop the Hammer on that Mean-Girl Culture!

I n her national bestseller, *Odd Girl Out: The Hidden Culture of Aggression In Girls*, Rachel Simmons gives us permission to grapple with the intricacies of girls and bullying. Many who read it might be tempted to confine a mean-girl culture and its traits to young girls navigating their way through school. However, we must be mindful of the fact that many of those same girls grow up to become mean women, especially when deep-seated issues remain unresolved.

A mean-girl culture is manifesting itself every day in the workplace. These women have yet to face the darkest parts of their experiences. Simmons' analysis helps to shed some light on how societal and psychological factors, among many others, contribute to a thriving mean-girl culture. Simmons shares this about the female experience, providing sharp insights into our journey across the years, and some of the foundations of a mean-girl culture: "Silence is deeply woven into the fabric of the female experience. It is only in the past thirty years that we have begun to speak the distinctive truths of women's lives, openly addressing rape, incest, domestic violence, and women's health. Although these issues always existed, over time we have given them a place in our culture by building public consciousness, policy, and awareness...Our culture refuses girls access to open conflict, and it forces their aggression into nonphysical, indirect, and covert forms. Girls use backbiting, exclusion, rumors, name-calling and manipulation to inflict psychological pain on victimized targets...girls frequently attack within tightly knit networks of friends, making aggression harder to identify and intensifying the damage to targets."

There are a number of grown up versions of these mean-girls in the workplace. Many women are still grappling with issues that happened decades ago—some of them may have even been the perpetrators. They carry years of both guilt and negative behavioral patterns. Others were the victims of horrible acts and, sadly, find themselves reliving these experiences in the workplace environment.

It's vital that we, as women in the workplace, go deeper in order to come to grips with mean-girl cultures and our own behavior.

Only then can we honestly call out these cultures through direct communication, grow from our experiences and help other women to thrive.

In this chapter, I highlight this behavior and provide practical approaches to offer help, should you have the misfortunate of encountering this. It's important to understand the various profiles of a mean-girl in the workplace. She may show up as a peer, your direct report, or even as your own manager. As one who has worked for over 25 years, I've seen many variations of this behavior. Further, I've had firsthand experience with these types of behaviors. They posed great challenges for me at varying times throughout my career. They have also taught me vital lessons. And, ultimately, they have caused me to grow, both personally and professionally, as I found my way through those situations. I share this with the same intention for you. Two things before reading on: *1) these behaviors described are obviously not exclusive to women. I highlight them because they exemplify a mean-girl culture, and are important to dissect in order to learn from, and 2) there are many profiles of this behavior, but I believe these to be among the more prevalent, based upon my experience.*

7 Profiles of a Mean-Girl

Profile #1: Sweet in Private, Mean in Public

She appears to be warm and gracious in private settings. She is the one who will always ask about your weekends, remembers the names of your children and dogs, and has very helpful advice about restaurants or great books to read. In public settings, however, she has a remarkable ability to switch personalities. She is cold and unsupportive during meetings. When it's time for you to make a presentation (which you've generously shared with her in private), she barely makes eye contact with you. Her comments about your work or ideas in those public settings are neutral at best, and critical at worst.

Profile #2: Character Assassin

She is adept at turning natural disagreements or disconnects into character issues. For example, rather than focus on the substance of a conversation or work product, she will be more likely to speak to your intentions. She will take great pains to accuse you of dishonesty or other nefarious deeds with little to no evidence. She is also quite liberal with her criticisms of your character, often engaging others in negative conversations about you.

Profile#3: The Public Shamer

She is given to public displays of intemperance, has unbridled emotions, and can be downright rude. In broader group settings, retreats, meetings or team sessions—she will launch into attack mode over the slightest issues. She is the person who will work brazenly to embarrass and humiliate you in front of others as she believes that this will score points with her peers, next level leaders, or advance her own warped agenda. The only good news about this profile is that she readily shows her true colors.

Profile #4: A Fake Friend

She is much like the first profile of one who is sweet in private and mean in public. However, a fake friend is far worse. She is adept at establishing herself as bona fide. Perhaps the two of you have gone to dinner together, and even shared a mani-pedi experience. She works to become familiar with your personal information, likes, dislikes, etc. in order to use that data for her own purposes. Have a sick father? Perhaps, she'll say to others, that you're not as available for a key project since you have to be out of the office to take care of your personal issues. This is one of the worst profiles of a mean-girl because she is able to reel you in, then expose and exploit your vulnerabilities.

Profile #5: A Powder Keg of Repressed Anger

She is ready to blow at any moment. She sits in meetings with a perpetual scowl on her face. You never quite know what has set her off. She takes several minutes to warm up in those meetings, initially offering no input and avoiding eye contact. As the meeting progresses, she may begin to contribute, but her comments will always contain thinly veiled sarcasm and will be focused more on demonstrating her own knowledge. She always has something to prove. You will frequently be on the other end of her anger, particularly if it's clear that you are a high performer. And, when meetings end, this mean-girl will rarely follow through on her commitments and may even work diligently to do the opposite of what she has promised. She's just plain angry.

Profile #6: An Eye-for-an-Eye Mentality

This mean-girl is after justice. She believes that slights against her—real or perceived—must be reckoned with. At times, those slights are really just disagreements which are commonplace in any work setting—however, she is more likely to take those things deeply personally. And, since direct confrontation is uncomfortable for her, she will seek her form of justice in insidious ways. She may visit HR, or your boss, to complain about you, raising issues which she has never shared directly with you.

Profile #7: Passive-Aggressive

Her behavior is the classic definition of passive-aggressive: indirect resistance or hostility through insults, other negative behavior, or inaction. However, in a mean-girl culture, this profile may offer a slight twist. Her penchant for indirect resistance or hostility may not necessarily have anything to do with her personal views about you. She could easily feel neutral, or even positive about you in some cases. However, this mean-girl moves in the direction which the wind is blowing—i.e., she bends with the changing dynamics of office politics. If she feels the need to align with the power structure against you, she'll never show it. Instead, she'll work in subtle and hard to decipher ways to thwart your efforts; looping you out of email chains, blind-copying your boss on communications, and any other creative way to make it more difficult for you to successfully advance your work.

These seven profiles are bleak renderings of grown up mean-girls in the workplace. They sound menacing but, take heart, there are strategies and skills to employ in navigating your way through this. In the process, you'll learn a lot about yourself and will be in a better position to strengthen your company's culture—if not your current one, then the next one. No company culture will ever be perfect because we, as individuals, are all imperfect. But, we can become more skillful in addressing these behaviors, and drop the hammer on these nasty cultures.

Before we get into the strategies and approaches to dealing with this behavior, I'd like to lovingly challenge some of you. It is possible that you are describing your company as having a mean-girl culture when, in reality, the issue is your own self-esteem, ability to accept constructive criticism or feedback, and/or your own sense of happiness. Before you label the company for which you work, or a particular situation as one of a mean-girl culture, engage in some honest self-reflection.

- When is the last time you received tough feedback about your performance or behavior? How do handle this kind of feedback, typically? Being on the receiving end of tough feedback is not easy, whether shared by your manager or a peer. But, you owe it to yourself to digest what's being said and look inwardly for ways to grow and develop, particularly if you aspire to go to new career levels. If you're unable to do this, you will go through each feedback experience feeling like a victim. That sense of victimization will cause you to feel attacked when you receive feedback which may actually be intended to help you.

- How well do you deal with disagreements and conflicts? Many women have great difficulty in managing conflict. There are many studies which confirm the high importance which women place on relationships. This, coupled with the societal mores on female behavior and direct confrontation, result in a strange elixir of individuals who will go to great lengths to avoid conflict and disagreements. In the workplace, we need disagreements. We need healthy debates and divergent opinions to get to the best solutions. Without this, groupthink takes hold and innovation is stifled. If you struggle with conflict and would prefer if everyone could all just get along, then you will view every workplace problem, challenge, or issue as owing to a mean-girl culture.

- Are you happy at work? Perhaps you are part of the meager 32% of the American workforce which, according to Gallup, is considered engaged (involved, committed, enthusiastic).[10] If you're not, then you have a lot of company, unfortunately. This also means that you are more likely than not to view every day at work as a necessary evil. You tolerate your coworkers rather than partner with them. And, since you've lost the energy and drive to be there, you may very well misinterpret normal work challenges and interactions as mean-girl behavior.

10 Approaches and Strategies to Overcoming Mean-Girl Behavior

Now that you've done some self-reflection, let's look at 10 approaches and practical strategies to deal with true mean-girl behavior which may be running rampant within a toxic corporate culture.

#1 Don't take it personally. I've already shared this, but it bears repeating—hurt people, hurt other people. We are all imperfect beings. We struggle through pain and disappointments. For those of us who have been through even darker times in our lives, the downstream effect of that pain is often felt by everyone with whom we come in contact—unless we go through a complete healing process. When we don't heal, we hurt. When we don't reconcile our past, we hurt. When we harbor unforgiveness, we hurt. So, needless to say, there are a whole lot of people who are hurting. What's worse, is that hurting people can quickly become infectious in all of the wrong ways. They are quick to react in anger, are distrustful, become easily threatened, and will rarely accept accountability for their actions—if they even grasp the impact of their actions to begin with. So, it's important to start with the understanding that the workplace includes damaged individuals, many of whom were part of mean-girl environments growing up. You may be among them, and if so, you may need to be both a giver and receiver of grace. If you're on the receiving end of mean-girl behavior in the workplace, avoiding the tendency to take things personally will help you to focus on the strategies—not the person—to combat it. You'll need to be sober-minded to deal with it. Otherwise, the emotional toll will be even greater.

#2 Remember who you are. Whether you bring 2 years or 20 years to your current company, you got the job because you were impressive during the interview. You beat out countless other candidates. Your unique skills and talents became obvious enough to your employer for you to receive an offer. You have credentials which set you apart. At some point, you defined goals and achieved a level of performance against those goals which further demonstrated your abilities. I'm quite sure that it won't take you long to remember the best accolades you have received from individuals whom you trust and respect. You are a daughter, mother, sister, niece, aunt or friend. There are people in your life who think highly of you. You have had an impact on them, and perhaps many others. You may even carry the banner of 'cancer survivor.' You may have come through transformative periods in your life—and you're the better for it. You are loved. You have not yet arrived at your final destination; you are on route to your destiny. Never forget that—and don't allow anyone to convince you that your circumstances define you. They do not.

#3 Increase your overall company value. Re-read Chapter 2 for ways to increase the value of the gift which you represent in the workplace. Beyond those strategies, it will be important to look for ways to become more engaged and involved in your workplace. When you're the victim of mean-girl behavior, you'll need as many advocates as you can find. You'll benefit from the help of individuals who: 1) have no horse in the race, 2) have a generosity of spirit, and 3) have influence of some sort. This may mean raising your hand to participate in a taskforce focused on a strategic initiative, joining a culture committee, or volunteering to support a project that is under-resourced. Do something beyond the norm to increase your overall value and put yourself on the radar of others who may be able to support you and help to mitigate your circumstances.

#4 Kill them with kindness. This strategy speaks directly to the importance of not personalizing someone else's bad behavior, as I shared earlier. But, killing the culprit with kindness asks far more of you than de-personalization, and it's incredibly difficult to do. It is unlikely that you'll find this switch quickly or consistently. But, here's the key—do it anyway. The harder you work to return the mean-girl behavior with even-tempered, polite and professional actions—the easier it will become. At first, you'll be doing it as a form of self-righteous judgment. Outwardly, you'll be kind, but inwardly you'll continue to hold onto your anger. It's hard not to. But, if you're committed to your emotional-well-being and sense of peace, you'll continue to work at this until it becomes easier, and more organic. Not only will you have successfully de-personalized the behavior, but you'll begin to see the perpetrator for who they are—someone who needs help. From there, you'll realize that there will be no exchange of kindness for your actions, and you will stop expecting it. Once you reach this point—with lots of practice—your energies can be better spent on the other strategies below.

#5 Kill them with your high performance. Rather than spend precious time obsessing about the next attack which you'll suffer at the hands of a mean-girl, work on your own game—your skills, that is. Invest in your own performance by doing everything possible to operate with excellence. Raise the bar on yourself and, once you've cleared it, raise it again. Go above and beyond your manager's expectations (see Chapter 2 for ideas) as you look to enhance your performance. This is always smart to do, and it will make it that much harder for a mean-girl in the workplace to hinder your success or accomplishments. Just be prepared: the stronger you perform, the more you can expect 'haters' to come out of the woodwork. But, you know what they say about haters—let them be your motivators!

#6 Use the experience to serve as a role model. As a woman aspiring toward greatness, you will always be surrounded by others who will be watching you closely. Once you begin to make strides in positive directions, achieve any notable success, etc., you'll become a role model—whether you've asked for this mantle or not. Younger female workers may begin to emulate your behavior when it becomes clear that you're onto something. Why is this important? Because, not only do you want to help others get to new levels, but you want to equip those newbies with the right tools to achieve their own version of success. If you're under attack and struggling through a toxic workplace culture, it's more important than ever not to allow your experience to taint others—particularly if you're in a management role. Demonstrate confidence and leadership, and others will have confidence in you, even when it's clear that things are not going so well. Stay positive, to the extent humanly possible. The team members around you—if they have any integrity themselves—will reward this trust with open communication and by continuing to bring their A-games to work every day. Exhibit integrity, even when you don't feel like it. If you're struggling through the craziness of a mean-girl culture, you will be more inclined to make decisions that are in your own best interest. Self-preservation is necessary. However, if you're making decisions in your own interests and those interests happen to run counter to those of your company—you've lost a piece of your integrity and the mean-girl behaviors have gotten the better of you. Keep this in mind as you're going through this. Capture your thoughts in a journal. Do anything that will help you to stay mindful of how important it is to walk in integrity.

#7 Use the experience as a developmental opportunity. Perhaps this experience will, down the road, give birth to a mentorship opportunity for you to give as a gift to someone else. Or, maybe it will be the foundation of a class that you teach, or book that you write in the future. You never know. So, stay open to learning and growing from the experience—even if it means some discomfort. If we can lean in to the kind of discomfort caused by dysfunctional cultures, the lessons in our own behavior, and that of others, will begin to crystallize. Honesty and authenticity in your own behavior matter here. If you're having a horrific week and have a few extra days off to spare, take them if you can. One of the best ways to develop and grow is to unplug and recharge your batteries. You'll be able to assess what's working, what's not, and seize a few *ah-ha* moments in times of solitude and reflection.

#8 Protect your personal business. I shared earlier that one way in which some mean-girls are able to wreak so much havoc in your life is when they discover more about you (see Profile #4). The workplace can be a tricky place for friendships. While you certainly want and need to build relationships, I've always erred on the side of privacy. It's true that there are many BFFs operating happily at work. However, just recognize that leaving yourself open to having close friends also increases the chances of your personal information becoming part of the company grapevine. This may sound cynical, and that's because it is. I believe it's important to maintain a healthy dose of cynicism when it comes to sharing your personal information at work. Here's a starter list for what you should never discuss at work: your finances, sex-life, relationship issues, health issues, politics, religion, or plans to quit. This is information that can, surreptitiously, be used to sow discord, create gossip, or otherwise malign you by the more skillful mean-girls found in the workplace.

#9 Choose your confidantes well, or don't choose them at all. Dealing with challenges in the workplace naturally creates a strong desire to vent. Venting helps to offload anger and frustrations. It can also uncover solutions. The truth is, you can't suffer in complete silence. Unfortunately, the higher up you get in the corporate ranks, the lonelier it will be. Confidantes must be both trusted to have your back and to have shown a degree of trustworthiness in the past. They may indeed exist in your orbit. But, even if you choose a confidante carefully and begin to share your problems openly with them, you will be vulnerable to outright betrayals—or even well-intentioned leaks that could come back to bite you. Aside from exceptional circumstances, it's best to use a spouse, friend outside of work, coach—or even your mother—to help you to vent and process what you're going through.

#10   Confront that monster-girl. Many of us would rather not have to face the mean-girl in a direct confrontation. It carries its risks. The conversation could get emotional and she could become further unhinged. She is likely to go on the defensive creating an even more unpredictable situation for you. But, the truth is, if it's clear that a conversation must be had, avoiding it will only cause the situation to deteriorate further. Those types of courageous conversations are important to both solving issues and to your own professional growth. If it's obvious that this type of conversation is necessary— don't run from it. There are ways to increase the odds of having a more productive conversation when confronting a mean-girl: 1) have your facts buttoned up; review them more than once, 2) play out scenarios for how she might react and then think about your responses to them, 3) role-play with a trusted individual before having the conversation, 4) during the conversation, fight the tendency to over-talk and over-explain. And, don't whine—just talk. Be deliberate about pausing after making each of your points. Deal with the awkward silence to allow your point to sink in and not become muddied in extra words, and 5) prepare yourself to receive unexpected feedback from her that may, or may not, be informative or useful. You can always decide later what to do with that feedback.

When all else fails, it may in fact be time to take your authentically awesome self elsewhere. I know that this may be easier said than done. There are so many voices in your head which will fight against making a final decision to move on: concerns about income, self-esteem, what others think of you, confusion about what's next, etc. One of the most pivotal moments in your career will be when you actually sit down and take a sober assessment of where you are and where you truly want to be. Your decision to move on should come down to this: is what you're experiencing worth it? Consider how you feel about the mission, leadership, ability to be your authentic self, growth opportunities, and where the company draws the line— or doesn't—around behaviors. If those assessments are still mostly positive, it may be worth sticking it out. But, if not, it's likely time to move on. Make the call and prepare for new opportunities, which are just waiting for you to show up. (I share more about job transitions in Chapter 7.)

Many of the strategies to deal with mean-girl behavior can work. It is possible for you to thrive—either temporarily or longer-term—in spite of this culture. There may be other factors which can work in your favor—i.e., a supportive manager, influential peers, or an organizational change.

But, mean-girl cultures can sap your spirit. If you're not careful, they can sour you and cause you to carry the negative baggage of the past into your future.

So, be intentional about assessing how much you're willing to tolerate. There's no time to waste. The world needs your skills and talents. You will be of no use to anyone if you're stuck in a toxic environment, unable to bring your best to the table.

Tough As Nails · Big Ideas

✓ The 7 profiles shared of mean girls in a workplace setting, are among the more common with which you should become familiar (pgs. 45-48)

✓ Highlighting these profiles enables us to call them out, and learn from them

✓ Consider whether your own self-esteem, ability to receive feedback, and happiness at work may be the real issues— rather than a mean-girl culture

✓ There are 10 approaches and practical strategies to dropping the hammer on mean-girl behavior. Refer to them prior to crafting an exit strategy (pgs. 50-58)

✓ When all else fails, you'll need to make a carefully calculated decision about how much you're willing to accept in dealing with mean-girl behavior

Pearls from Jo's Journal

The notion of remembering who you are when you're under attack within a toxic workplace, can't be overstated. We need other people to remind us of this, particularly when we're at our weakest. We needn't wait for our circumstances to turn negative before we're prompted to remember who we are and the value we bring. These times of reflection should always be welcomed. I carry a treasured memory with me of having left an organization several years ago to move on to another opportunity. At my farewell get-together, I received a lovely gift—which would have been more than enough for me. But, that wasn't the best part of the experience. I also received a small gift box with 23 little slips of paper placed inside. Each slip of paper contains a special expression of admiration about my leadership or actions, which clearly made indelible impressions on team members during my tenure at this organization. I call them my love notes. They are incredibly inspiring. On days when I am tempted to forget who I am, deluged by negativity, I take out that gift box...and remember.

Chapter 5

Healthier Leadership Models

L ife in the workplace is full of all kinds of pressure: the pressure to perform, the pressure to lead, the pressure to be led—and on and on. You never know what's waiting for you at the office on any given day.

There's also a different kind of pressure which you will face as you move through your career—the pressure to give 150% of your energies and commitment to work. This kind of pressure is unreasonable. The fallacy around giving 150% as a sign of commitment begins at the very earliest stages of your career.

The need to be perceived as committed to your job will draw you—slowly, steadily and stealthily—into always being 'on' and available to an employer. Periodic days off or longer vacations where you wish to be fully relieved of your obligations in order to enjoy time with your family, often test both your own self-discipline and your employer's culture. The spoken and unspoken expectations which define what it means to be the 'ideal employee,' tend to result in unsustainable work habits. For the majority of employers, being 'on' is a demonstration of loyalty.

What results is a leader who neither has it all, nor is she effectively doing it all. This harried leader offers a very distinct and poor model to those aspiring to greatness: pack your calendar with as many meetings as humanly possible; lurch from appointment to appointment with no breaks in between; construct a super-human travel schedule; and dive in and out of situations (which clearly require more thoughtful interactions) to demonstrate how indispensable you are. These leaders *are* actually 'on' all the time, even as they give lip-service to other employees about the need for a better work/life balance. Consciously or unconsciously, they shape the path for others striving to be noticed. There are obviously exceptions to these types of employers and leaders—but, not yet enough of them to truly change this paradigm.

The model of leadership which I've described above is not only unhealthy, but it leaves little bandwidth or energy to think about anything else outside of work. Under that model, you will be working hard, but not smart. You will be busy, but often unproductive. Your days will be long and lacking focus. This self-defeating leadership model will mean that the 'allowable' time for you to tap into your creativity, explore hobbies or other interests will be greatly reduced, if not altogether eliminated.

Women rising to the top, or already there, have a wonderful opportunity to develop new hammers and new nails to add to their personal toolkits.

They can chart a different course—a *very* different model of leadership for others to follow.

The first step involves choosing your time wisely—which means exercising the power to say 'no' without guilt or equivocation. When we say 'yes' to something, we could be saying 'no' to something more important. Once you develop the ability to be more discriminating with your time, you can then more effectively focus on your own leadership development.

Over the years, I've built a mini-library of 6 traits which I describe as *Jo's Radical Leadership Trait Theory*. I don't describe these traits as 'radical' because they are extreme in practice. They are traits necessary for breakthrough leadership. Yet, they are still rare, based upon my experience in the workplace. So, the 'radical' descriptor is more of a reflection of my belief that they are too often an extreme departure from the far more common, and far less effective, leadership seen among many in positions of power. As leaders, we all need to work intentionally to develop these skills and behaviors through personal reflection, mentors, coaching programs, courses, and on-the-job experiences. In Chapter 3, I spent quite a bit of time on 'decision-making' as one of the traits, as I feel strongly that this is vital for leaders—especially female leaders—to master. In this section I share all 6 of them, in no particular order, along with descriptions of the necessary competencies. They are key to successfully navigating the rough terrains of unpredictable and challenging business landscapes.

Jo's 'Radical' Leadership Trait Theory

1. High Emotional Intelligence
Demonstrates thoughtful responses to challenging and complex issues and people

- She enthusiastically and fearlessly embraces new experiences or ideas. She engages other perspectives freely, and is comfortable having her beliefs challenged. She has the humility to embrace the fact that there is always more that she can learn.

- She demonstrates empathy towards others. She is more forgiving of her own flaws and those of others.

- She has incredible self-awareness, and an awareness of others. Her grasp of verbal and non-verbal communication and listening skills is remarkable; and is able to interact effectively with others.

- She is resilient and does not internalize failure—at least, not for long. Instead, she embraces the pain from past mistakes in order to become stronger and smarter—readily sharing that information with others.

2. Risk-Taker
Employs safety nets, but is not tethered to them; is able to take smart leaps

- She fully understands the power of data to assess trends, patterns and predictability. She combines that data with the human aspects.

- She has developed an array of tools and frameworks to make small and large-scale decisions.

• She can hold two competing thoughts in her head at once, ferreting out what is and isn't important between them as she moves toward action. Action is never avoided.

• She loves data but can operate in gray areas, recognizing and accepting the downsides of her decisions.

3. Relentless Decision-Maker
Not afraid to advance the ball, or give it to others

• She understands what decisions are important to make; and she can distinguish between small routine decisions, and big, high-impact decisions.

• She is comfortable owning the decision, or being clear about who does.

• She is laser-focused on making a few decisions with excellence (positive results, timely, etc.) rather than a bunch of decisions poorly.

4. Authentic Truth-Teller
Will acknowledge the negatives with her own 'special sauce' way of talking and doing

• She is unafraid to be vulnerable and will express the 'ugly' in situations.

• She has few, if any, gaps between what she says and what she actually does.

• When she makes mistakes, she is honest about them and uses the opportunity to (re)build relationships.

• She communicates with precision, avoiding jargon and corporate-speak; others know exactly where they stand with her.

5. Transformational Thinker and Doer

Attracts and retains followers much like a magnet

- She leads with strong credibility and by example; her reputation precedes her.
- She doesn't hesitate to roll up her sleeves to get the job done at any level of the task at hand.
- She is deeply uncomfortable and skeptical of the status quo; always pushing the thinking to new levels.
- She inspires innovation in others and is adept at bringing disparate perspectives together.

6. A Balanced Leader

She uses a careful mix of leadership approaches, honing them along the way

- She brings her authentic self to the workplace, even as she grows personally and professionally.
- She works to avoid playing into the worst stereotypes of female leadership (see Chapter 3).
- She has wisely and strategically adopted a few of the skills and behaviors which her workplace brothers use deftly (see Chapter 3).

Exploring Interests Outside of One's Job

Now that I've painted a vivid picture of healthy leadership and given you something to which you can aspire, other nagging questions still remain: How can you bring *all* of yourself to work? Can you operate as a healthy leader and pursue your passions, other aspirations and interests? Should you even attempt to? Let's try to answer these questions by first reflecting on what your employer may have wanted to hear from you when you were a candidate for the position which you later accepted.

During the 'courting' period when you put your hat in the ring for that amazing opportunity, your employer may have asked you some interesting and probing questions: *'What do you enjoy doing when you're not at work?'*; *'What are your hobbies?'*; *'Do you have other interests outside of your field?'* All of these questions were designed to understand more of who you are. Why? Because they were looking for well-rounded individuals who could leverage their skills and thrive in a variety of settings. It was appealing to them to know that you were involved in other areas that demonstrated your leadership skills, desire to grow, ability to set goals, and had outlets for your passions as a wonderfully complex person. So, is it possible that that same employer could now expect you to stifle your other interests in order to focus myopically on your day job?

I'm afraid so. The pressure on companies to do more with less, to win, to stay financially solvent, and to outperform others may cause them to change their original philosophies in this area. If that happens, be prepared for this to create another unwanted kind of pressure for you to deal with. It is the kind of pressure which will hamper your ability or desire to bring all of yourself to work. In that circumstance, your pursuit of outside interests may even be viewed as disloyal by some employers. However, there's a truth that runs counter to that.

We are complex and multi-faceted human beings, with a rainbow of goals, dreams and interests.

Women, in particular, increase diversity well beyond our gender. We possess an ability to introduce different ways of thinking and working to get results. We are known to be adept at juggling and multitasking—able to thoughtfully give our attention to more than one thing at a time. In a statement made by Svetlana Kuptsova, one of the authors of a 2016 study on sex and age-related characteristics of brain functioning during task-switching, published in Human Physiology, the nuances of this multitasking were revealed. According to the author, the study's findings suggest that "women might find it easier than men to switch attention, and their brains do not need to mobilize extra resources in doing so as opposed to male brains." In layman's terms, this means that women have a natural tendency and comfort level with managing disparate tasks and information as a normal part of our lives. I'm hard-pressed to believe that those same skills wouldn't apply to effective juggling on a larger scale—among our day jobs, hobbies and other pursuits.

As long as your performance and results on the job aren't being sacrificed, it behooves an employer to find ways to tap into *every* dimension of your inherent skills, background, experiences and interests. If you volunteer at other organizations, or are building relationships and networks in other arenas, you can bring invaluable resources and contacts to your employer. That's what I would describe as a *win-win*.

Of course, you should always be responsible and diligent enough to ensure that other activities don't violate your company's conflict of interest policies. Reviewing your employee handbook for any 'moonlighting' clauses which restrict activities outside of work, is wise. Consulting an attorney for advice regarding gray areas may also be prudent. Once it's clear that your intentions are pure and that your activities can be performed without detriment to your work responsibilities, a little creativity on the part of your employer can go a long way. If you're a budding entrepreneur, you could be sitting on the next hottest idea—which your company may be able to benefit from in some form, if they have enough foresight. Perhaps you can take a few months off, unpaid, with the agreement that you will return by a certain date. Or, maybe you can work part-time to devote the needed time to a new venture while not fully relinquishing your day job. Across many industries, combining full-time or part-time work and self-employment is seen as the future workforce.

It's no secret that, in this digital age, work and personal time have never been more blurred due to technology enablers. It comes down to whether your company demonstrates trust in their employees. If they do, then you may be able to partner with your manager to arrange a schedule which allows you to execute your responsibilities while leaving you the flexibility to explore other interests. If not, you have a couple of other avenues.

Get creative yourself. Again, this is not to suggest that you operate in any way other than fully committed to your employer and through adherence to company policies. Once that is the case, there is nothing that should prevent you from using your paid time off days, evenings (when possible) and weekends to pursue other interests and projects.

Look for other company cultures which have been 'upgraded' to new ways of work. As you search for opportunities at other companies (provided that you don't become a full-time entrepreneur), add flexible work arrangements (i.e. flexible hours, compressed workweeks, telecommuting) to your 'must-have' list as you identify the right employer.

Finally, whether or not you're able to explore other interests outside of the workplace is heavily dependent upon your ability to operate under a healthy model of leadership during working hours. Commit to operating as a 'radical' leader who exercises healthy behaviors so that you'll have more room for that exploration.

Tough As Nails · Big Ideas

✓ Consciously, or unconsciously, leaders who are always 'on' are shaping a poor model of leadership for others

✓ You can shape a very different leadership model through healthier behaviors and the power of saying 'no'

✓ There are 6 vital leadership traits necessary for breakthrough leadership (pgs. 66-68)

✓ It behooves employers to tap into every dimension of your skills and interests—for their benefit as much as for yours

✓ Get creative in exploring outside interests—i.e. use your time-off and weekends

✓ Be a 'radical' leader who exercises healthy behaviors, and you'll have more room for exploration outside of your day job

Pearls from Jo's Journal

As someone who considers herself a bit of a leadership geek, I find myself observing leadership behaviors all the time— everywhere. We all have access to endless blueprints for what strong leadership looks like. And, many of us have read about leaders who neglected to learn important lessons from those before them who made mistakes and missteps. From the internet, to mentors, to coaches, to the gazillion books and articles written on the subject—there is much to glean from. We can easily tailor those blueprints to fit our styles, personal philosophies, etc. So, if we choose not to learn or to make any adjustments as a leader—especially a leader of other people— that is essentially doing the same thing in the same way, yet expecting different results. Hmmm...I think there's a name for that...

Chapter 6

Have a Wide Assortment of Tools

You'll be more successful if you possess—and are able to deploy—a wide assortment of business tools in any given business situation. A clear value proposition, customer loyalty, finding and keeping the right talent, and risk mitigation are among the multitude of areas in which companies must excel on a daily basis. Rising to the occasion will demand versatility.

I've been in work environments when one moment we were embarking on a strategic plan—which may have been a natural continuation of the previous strategy—and the next, we found ourselves reeling from unanticipated forces in the market, forcing us to scrap everything in front of us. I've also experienced the swings of a change in strategies that were driven by financial constraints—i.e., escalating costs, weak revenue streams, etc. The skills and mindset which you need to maintain equilibrium and stay afloat during tumultuous times, are very different than those needed to simply maintain the status quo. As a leader, you will need to be comfortable with operating within a variety of environments. As you progress in your career, others will assume that you have these skills and you'll become a role-model—either for how to manage challenges, or how *not* to.

These unrelenting business challenges, require the toughest and most savvy leaders to operate much like chameleons. Chameleons (the actual ones) are highly specialized lizards with over 200 species, many of them possessing the ability to change colors as they adapt to their surroundings and/or signal their intentions. It's already well known that they can change colors. What's not as well known, is the fact that they can change in as little as 20 seconds. Sometimes, the change in color allows the chameleon to communicate with other chameleons. Do any of these traits sound useful in today's business climates? 'Changing colors', in our world, simply means flexing with the demands of changing business environments. If you wish to become an influential leader, you'll need to add this ability to your repertoire. As you do, you should also remain mindful of, and sensitive to your company's current climate.

Remember the *Why*

If the top leader can't instill a clear purpose for your company's mission, strategies, and goals, they obviously should not be in that role. But, assuming the purpose is in fact clear, it's your job to help keep it alive—especially during periods of change when the company is more vulnerable to confusion.

At some point during your tenure, either at your current or past company, you fully bought into the purpose—the 'why' of that company's existence. You were also excited about their espoused values. I hope that this is still the case for you today.

However, the reality is that many companies may not always live up to their ideals and may struggle to clearly articulate their purpose through times of uncertainty. That's where strong leadership—at all levels—makes a tremendous difference. If you're in the midst of a major organizational restructuring and are experiencing unwanted turnover among some key roles— it's a perfect time for you to return to your company's strategy and value statements. That will remind you and your colleagues of the original purpose and help to regain focus, as these difficult times will serve as great tests of character. As a leader, you should set yourself apart by demonstrating what effective leadership looks like during these times. For example, if one of your company's value statements is about 'bold leadership', you can be an example of that value at the next business meeting. Be courageous as you offer a different perspective related to a business strategy. It may actually help the stakeholders in the room to move towards a clearer decision. Bringing a sense of the array of possibilities and some boldness to the table also empowers others to follow suit—and to remember why they are there.

Encourage Employees to Row in the Same Direction

Employees need other employees to sharpen them. At times, that sharpening is made more difficult due to infighting and an 'us' versus 'them' mentality. When conflicts aren't handled directly, office politics will take over in full force. This, in turn, causes routine activities to devolve into finger-pointing, lack of accountability and decision-making driven by covering one's rear end. Emails become the tool of choice for every simple communication within this kind of dysfunctional climate, where every team member and their great uncle is copied. Meetings become havens of opaque conversations, nefarious glances across the table, and withheld information. Some of the company's leaders may begin to treat each other like the enemy, effectively taking their eyes off of the true marketplace competitors. In efforts to seize control and increase power, some leaders will even engage other influencers to push their personal strategy *du jour*, taking the entire company down a rabbit hole. Resistance will be met with passive aggression and disruptive management styles which are used to retain power. These employees and leaders will forget—or may not care— that infighting doesn't produce better outcomes nor does it solve pressing problems. Self-inflicted damage will begin to occur where the company's precious people resources are spending the majority of their workweeks battling each other, instead of the real business challenges facing them. The domino effect of this behavior is demonstrable—i.e. employee absenteeism, sick leaves, unwanted turnover. There are ways for you to lead through this, using your own authentic voice.

- Change what you can control. When you adjust the thermostat in the basement, it's not changing the temperature in the upstairs living room. Think of the office environment in the same way. You can't control everything, but there are some areas in which you can have an impact. When you hear the latest piece of gossip or rumors swirling around the workplace, choose a different set of behaviors. Remind people of where to go to clarify rumors. While you can listen to complaints, be sure to respond with actionable solutions.

• Inspire benefit-of-the-doubt thinking. When someone in the office engages you in a conversation about an employee's behavior, empower them to be the author of both that story and its outcome. Help them reframe the issue and think about how they can handle the situation—and the person—differently. After a while, people will begin to visit you for more than venting, they will want to glean from your wisdom as they develop their own problem-solving skills. You will be a pivotal voice in the workplace.

• Turn the conversation from 'they' to 'we' at every opportunity. Language and words really matter. The words which one chooses to convey her thoughts have great influence over the interpretation and actions taken by others. You can be a leader in creating company unity by that one simple word—'we.' It will help to break down both artificial and real silos, reminding people of the importance of operating under one culture.

• Infect the space with optimism. A positive attitude can easily spread to others. Not only does it spread, but it also sucks the air out of negativity. Words of encouragement, new ideas, support for projects, and sharing resources are all ways to demonstrate positivity. At some point, these actions will put a spotlight on others who are working in contrast to these ideals.

Help the C-Suite Regain Their Footing

A healthy C-Suite team is one of the key ingredients to a company's success, especially during times of change and uncertainty. The signs of poor health among an executive team are often quite difficult to pinpoint, as the potential sources of the problem can be varied. However, your ability to uncover the issues hobbling an executive team will have far-reaching impact on the entire organization. The advice in this section is particularly for those of you who are either part of the C-Suite, or those who have an opportunity to operate as coaches to C-Suite members. Perhaps you're the top human resources officer, or a senior level HR professional who can advise a willing CEO. Or, you may be serving on the board of directors and can influence the leadership from that vantage point. As you work to shed light on key business issues, suggest course corrections to current strategies and provide other types of support to the leaders at the top of the house—there are a few 'C-Suite problem-scenarios' which you should be aware of as you offer solutions.

- High performing individuals will not necessarily be successful on an executive team. It may be puzzling to see a C-Suite team in disarray when its members, by most accounts, are described as top talent. The fact is, there are leaders who have fabulous skills and amazing intellect who may be better utilized as taskforce members or individual contributors.

- There are times when the mandate of the executive team may need to shift. You may have started the fiscal year on stable ground, but are now in a period of major restructuring, downsizing, or in desperate need of a turnaround. Conversely, you could be on an upward trajectory where your company is now positioning itself to scale key programs across multiple geographies. When the overall mandate shifts, the quality and quantity of executive skill sets will be on full display. Expertise in areas such as change management, public presentations, stakeholder management and technological savvy will no longer be desirable—they will be required. At a senior level, this may mean executive coaching support, or 'buying' talent in order to fill internal performance gaps. One of the most detrimental things a company can do to any business is to ignore major skills gaps at the executive level. You can be the one to call this out if you sense avoidance in this area. Just be sure to do so with diplomacy—focusing on the skill set, not the individual.

• Some executive teams are too large, or poorly constructed. Over time, it is possible that an executive team will become somewhat like Frankenstein's monster, operating disjointedly and oddly configured. In efforts to stroke egos, a CEO may retain members on the executive team who have unclear or informal leadership roles, and who participate inconsistently in key meetings. In other cases, an inability to make difficult decisions which require differentiating among leaders may result in too large of a team. This reduces the team's ability to be nimble at a time when that trait is desperately needed. There are many models of executive teams—some can even be shaped temporarily to address the urgencies of the moment. It may be helpful to work with the CEO to experiment with different team models which are fluid, yet clearly defined.

- Everyone is in the room, yet no one seems to be leading. This scene plays out every day at company meetings and during board presentations. Executives with overlapping job descriptions are assembled to advance a business initiative, yet the conversation as to who owns what has never been held. The VP of Business Development may be tripping over the Managing Director of Acquisitions who, in turn, is not sure how to work with the new Head of Strategy. Confusion and disconnects arising during the executive team meetings are almost always symptomatic of a larger problem. It's best that when you do highlight these disconnects among executive roles, you ensure that your recommendations include much broader organizational design changes. Any adjustments to individual roles and titles will inevitably have a downstream effect on the respective teams under each executive leader.

- Some executive teams may be suffering from a classic 'bunker mentality.' It's tough to admit when you've gone off course. It's *really* tough when those strategic mistakes are costing the company revenue, donors, talent and/or its reputation. An executive team lost in groupthink (see Chapter 1) needs a truth-teller among them who isn't afraid to call out flawed strategies. All companies are vulnerable to stumbling, and all of them *will* at some point. A bunker mentality, a term derived from the actual experience of military defenses, is evident when members of a team will resist ideas and default to extreme defensiveness when challenged. In the bunker, actions must be justified at all costs. Admissions of mistakes—small and large—are frowned upon. A bunker mentality among executive teams who are loath to acknowledge their troubles, manifests itself in several ways: leaders are afraid to lead and will run every action up, down and across every flagpole; everything will be a priority and their teams will be afraid to say 'no'; key decisions will be treated more like hot potatoes, bouncing from one part of the company to the other; and green-lighted decisions will mysteriously run into red-lights. The company in this scenario is, essentially, in a state of paralysis. Its leaders have chosen to believe their own headlines and are rejecting any data which contradicts their current direction—or they may be bending that data to fit accordingly. They need someone unafraid to share the 'ugly.' You have a golden opportunity to be that individual. While not without its risks, it's a role that has the potential to save an entire company from decline. You can mitigate the risks of being this truthteller by: 1) seeking out other advocates, 2) de-personalizing conversations, and 3) approaching them with a solutions-orientation. Ultimately, whether they want to admit it or not, executives need help—they just want that help to come without overexposing their weaknesses.

Use the Chaos to Innovate

I've never seen groundbreaking ideas emerge from the same old ways of thinking. By definition, innovation requires newness. In times of chaos, particularly the type that is stoked internally by some of the dysfunctional behavior which I've described in this

Chapter, the opportunities to create, or re-create, are significantly multiplied. This will require you to tap into skill sets which you typically use outside of the workplace. If you're a mother, sister, friend, or daughter you've likely been managing risk, seizing opportunities, and leading with courage in your off hours. Those skills in problem-solving, creativity, and crisis-management should still be intact when you enter the office. Now, it's time to use them. They could be the keys to innovation, and may help to channel the chaos of your company into something constructive. Ask your manager to set aside time during your standing team meetings for brainstorming solutions to the company's thorny issues. Secure enough support from those with authority and influence in your company to pilot a low-risk idea for a new program or practice. This will also help you to build muscle in this area, and will get others comfortable with trying new things without the fear of experiencing a major failure. If you're in a position of management, you can lead the charge.

Think Outside of *Their* Box
This may be the most important concept to grasp during your entire professional life. If you are ever to stretch, grow and evolve as a leader, you must: 1) give yourself permission to step into your *dis*comfort zone, and 2) be intentional about thinking outside of the boxes in which others will try to place you. This type of 'chameleon thinking' benefits you personally, and will ultimately benefit your company.

Push beyond the traditional model of career development where careers are built over a span of time. Under a traditional model, one carefully builds their credentials—i.e. educational, experiential, relational—navigating their professional journeys through the requisite battle testing. Each stop along the way presents another opportunity to hold the all-important 'market value' conversations as salaries and appropriate compensation packages are negotiated before embarking upon the next rung of this climb. Ascending along this career ladder is the equivalent of acquiring more chips to play at the table in order to get to the next round—whatever that may be. We've been programmed to think of our career progress within these linear terms, methodically moving through giant hierarchies. There are other ways to think of career progression.

In a 2016 article posted on the BIE Executive blog entitled, *Why the Traditional Career Path Is No Longer Relevant,* Ettie McCormack, wrote that, "a career path is less about carefully plotted steps that must be taken in a particular order, and more about opportunities for growing knowledge through multiple experiences." Seeking out stretch assignments, or project work outside of your comfort zone are ways to develop a variety of experiences which can shape your career. When that work gives you a window into other parts of the business, your personal 'stock' has instantly risen, making you even more valuable to your company.

I've long been a proponent of career lattices over career paths, and rotational assignments over structured roles. They allow for the exploration of roles that can result in promotions, lateral moves or even steps backward needed to expand one's expertise. The possibilities found within more flexible thinking around careers, are endless. In addition, today's workforce is more diverse than ever, in every way. Teams are often partially or fully virtual, business units are geographically dispersed, workforces are comprised of multi-generational populations, and organizational structures are being shaped more creatively to fit the business direction. Teams that operate with fluidity and unencumbered by rigid structures, will always be better positioned to outperform their counterparts. As importantly, our personal growth and development depends upon a multitude of work experiences. This is what makes us tougher, more confident, and far more versatile leaders.

As one who has spent the bulk of her career in the field of human resources, I can attest to the fact that many employers are slow to look for ways to leverage and develop skills outside of the traditional career paths. HR professionals, for example, too often find themselves stuck in ruts where they are rarely viewed as viable candidates for other types of roles. The HR field is dominated by women—as many as 70%, by some estimates—yet, we're missing the opportunity to support broader career advancements for these women. Qualified women are suffocating underneath artificially imposed glass ceilings due to a lack of creative thinking among those with authority and influence. Can you imagine the leaps that would be made in gender diversity across the business world if even 20% of the women in HR—with a focus on the high potentials—were better positioned and supported to advance into other functional areas?

Boxed thinking is a loss for everyone in business. HR leaders, by necessity, will have honed skills in organizational development and business transformation—areas that companies covet and should be working to leverage. Many of those skills are readily transferable to other fields such as Strategy or Communications specializations.

The lesson here: you will need to be more assertive. Perhaps this means being tough-as-nails enough to raise your hand for other opportunities. Just be sure that you're willing to do the hard work required to take on new roles.

As you move through your career, think broadly. Be intentional about building your skills and experiences. Volunteer for the types of projects which will challenge you. Don't allow others to confine you to roles if you believe that you're capable of doing more. This posture will require thoughtful reflection and a few key considerations.

- Understand and acknowledge your underlying motivations. Are you looking for more money or more self-worth? It's certainly nice to have both, but what holds the deepest value to you? Are you being driven by a need to expand options due to a relocation? The answers matter, and will impact your career exploration choices greatly.

- Take stock of your skills, and the tools already acquired in your toolkit. How have they been applied over the years, and in what areas? For example, your facilitative leadership skills may have been used while in an HR role, but were applied in certain strategic settings which ultimately helped to move a business forward. That counts for something.

- Network, network, and keep networking. Your ability to meet the right people, associated with other 'right people', increases exponentially as you develop relationships.

• Set clear goals around your career explorations, chart out specific opportunities and take actions against them.

The best 'chameleons' among us have become adept at strategically shifting during times of change, leading the way during chaos, and morphing into other roles which increase their value and serve the business.

Identify those chameleons and learn from them.

Tough As Nails · Big Ideas

✓ As you progress in your career, you will either become a role-model for how to lead during change, or how *not* to

✓ Unrelenting business challenges require leaders who have an ability to operate with an incredibly wide assortment of business tools. These leaders can adapt to rapidly changing circumstances

✓ Work hard to keep your company's purpose and values alive during periods of change

✓ Be the leader who reminds others, through your own actions, about the importance of team unity

✓ There are several problem-scenarios which can hobble an executive team. Your ability to get to the root of them can have a major impact (pgs. 80-83)

✓ Some of the best groundbreaking ideas can come from tapping into skills which you use outside of the workplace

✓ If you are to stretch as a leader, you must step into your *dis*comfort zone and resist being boxed in by others

✓ As you move through your career, think broadly and unconventionally

Pearls from Jo's Journal

Over the years, I've really honed the skill of operating as a chameleon in the workplace. This has allowed me to raise my hand for a variety of assignments. I've also been asked to take on other roles—small and large—which were well outside of my own functional area. There's no doubt that this has added significant value to the teams and organizations of which I've been a member. I'm really proud of that. Yet, over the years, I came to discover something less pleasant that occurred, at times, in those circumstances: I wasn't always valued for being a chameleon. Sometimes the results which I achieved were ignored and attribution for my work was given to someone else. In some sense, this is understandable as a strong ability to adapt can be invisible, or less obvious to others. Being highly adaptable will increase our value, but we need to ensure that we're not being taken advantage of. That means speaking up when necessary—even when it may not be our natural inclination. Servant leadership, indeed, has its limits.

Chapter 7

You May Bend, But You Won't Break

You and your job *are* mutually exclusive. If you happen to lose your job, you have not lost yourself.

Job transitions happen frequently. American workers spend, on average, less than 5 years in any given job. In 2016, for the first time in over a decade, the Bureau of Labor Statistics reported a decline in employee tenure from 4.6 to 4.2 years, over a 2-year period.[11] This also means that there is a lot of time and energy being spent by people looking to transition to another position. The reasons behind that transition are many: layoffs; yours or the company's relocation; the need for work/life balance; outsourcing of a department; skill mismatches; toxic cultures—you name it. It happens. Most of us would agree with the first sentence in this Chapter, yet we may still struggle to draw a distinction between our personal identities and the positions which we hold. There is clear evidence of this fact. At social gatherings, I often hear answers to conversation-openers such as *'tell me more about yourself'* that are solely focused on the individual's job, title, or where s/he works. This is a trap that many of us will fall into if we're not careful. If you're intertwining 'self' and 'job', the loss of your employment will cause you to question yourself in unhealthy ways.

I recently asked Nancy Karas, Organizational Change Agent, Career Mentor and Master Coach, for her insights on how to think about the relationship between ourselves and our jobs. Nancy shared that "you must consider yourself an entity unto itself. You are your own organization, your own CEO. You take your expertise and talent with you from job to job. As we enter the gig economy, we must remember that if we lose our title and paycheck, we do not lose our substance. As the average length of service with each company hovers around 4.2 years, we must become experts at rebranding and marketing ourselves to showcase how we can add immediate and significant value to our next endeavor—whether that is a target organization, a consulting gig, or our own business or project."

Now, let's confront a cold truth: none of us is owed a job. The legal term 'at-will employment' largely takes care of any debate surrounding that question. Employers can dismiss their employees for any reason without having to establish just cause, so long as that reason is not illegal—i.e., discrimination. While we are not owed a job, we certainly expect our employers to operate with integrity, employ sound policies, take the time to address issues, and in the case of layoffs, to explore any feasible business alternatives before eliminating positions. When these expectations are not met, the job loss can be even more devastating. You may be tempted to look inwardly for the personal 'defect' which resulted in your termination. When, this happens, remember the first sentence in this Chapter: You and your job *are* mutually exclusive.

How do you 'find' yourself after losing a job which you've allowed to become entangled with your sense of identity and value? It's hard work. But, it is doable. You may bend through this process, but you won't break—we are all much stronger than we think.

Not All Job Losses Are Created Equal

After working in the human resources field for so many years, I understand quite a bit about one's emotional state and sense of professional recovery. Your emotions will differ depending upon the reason for the departure - all of this is very normal and you should give yourself the gift of acknowledging your emotions, not denying them. The key will be to focus on regaining your confidence, then returning to living life like a BOSS (more on that in Chapter 10). Before you refocus, it will help to dissect the experience so that you can learn lessons and move on as quickly as possible. Each type of job loss has its own takeaways.

- Layoffs due to restructuring, outsourcing or other business changes will happen frequently across every industry and type of business. The external climate demands that employers must sometimes make tough decisions. A need to establish different organizational designs, streamline functional areas, and employ other cost-containment opportunities will impact people—one way or the other. Understand, as difficult as it may be, that business decisions are typically not personal. Think of it this way: If you were planning to remodel your home to give it a significant upgrade, you would likely shop around to find a highly skilled tradesman beyond the typical handyman whom you may have previously employed to perform smaller jobs in your home. Your goal is to match the job with the precise expertise. That's just good business sense.

- Mismatches between your own brand of special sauce and a given role, are also common. It is possible that your philosophies and style of leadership could be an anathema to a particular company, resulting in the workplace version of 'irreconcilable differences.' Or, you may find that your particular skill sets are not the proper match for the role. If this happens, your chances of any real success or happiness are slim to none. Continuing to work under those circumstances is the equivalent of pushing a boulder uphill every day. Parting ways—whether it's your idea or your employer's—is a blessing in a not-so-subtle disguise. Your departure means that you will have been freed from a job that was not a role in which you could shine; where each day was probably a pretty miserable experience for you. You can now look for another opportunity that can better maximize your unique talents and expertise. And, there's more good news—if you don't waste the experience: you can glean lessons from what happened perhaps by doing a self-assessment of your performance and development areas. This could help to minimize the chances of future mismatches. It's often helpful to engage others in this navel-gazing stage, so that you come away with more objective takeaways. Enlist the help of a formal or informal coach who can give you feedback.

• Leaving a job because the workload and hours are close to killing you—figuratively or literally—makes complete sense. The much sought-after *work/life balance*, continues to be a worthy goal—though there is not a singular definition of what that balance looks like, especially for women trying to juggle multiple roles. What is clear, however, is that working insane hours, and living in a state of exhaustion will be short-lived. Continuing to stay could be the precursor to marital problems, major health issues, or other unwanted situations. No job on earth is worth that. When you make this important decision, you will be in the luxurious position of planning ahead for your departure. Repackaging your skills and taking a broad assessment of 'what's next' in your life is fun work, and could be incredibly rewarding. You can step back to ask yourself questions like: *What am I doing when I'm most energized? What would I want to spend my time doing, even if I didn't get paid for it? What gifts and talents do others typically compliment me on?* You will be wise to take the time to do this so that you can structure your exit accordingly.

• Toxic cultures can be soul-crushing, and you definitely need to keep your soul intact. Continuing to stay in a culture which is known internally, and in the external marketplace, for backbiting, distrust, mean-girl (and boy) behavior, and every other negative adjective—is unsustainable. Even the best manager may not be enough for you to tough it out in these kinds of cultures. And, in some cases, your manager could be toxic as well. If you tried to make this work with every interpersonal tool and strategy known to humankind, and are still suffering, then it's time to leave. If not, you might become part of the problem, or you will gradually join the nearly three quarters of staff who are reported to be disengaged at work. Both scenarios are incredible wastes of time and talent. So, review the advice in the bullets above, rinse then repeat.

Myths About Losing Your Job

I've already dealt with the largest and most nagging myth surrounding a job loss—that you and your job are intertwined. Not only is this a myth to be busted during a season of job loss, but it is important to remember when one is gainfully employed as well. It is vital that each of us does the work of securing an identity that is separate and apart from a job. Our sense of identity should be enveloped in our 'why's.' *Why am I here? Why do I gravitate towards, and find joy in, (you fill in the blank)?* For example, I believe that part of my purpose is to bring expressions of encouragement to other people—in my personal and professional life. I also believe that part of my purpose is to help other people—especially women—to find, and understand more fully, their own purpose. That can manifest itself in many ways well outside of any 9am-5pm role that I'm in. I can engage in women's ministry programs, leadership activities and even informal chats at a grocery store. When we understand our 'why's', we are no longer tethered to things upon which our self-identity should not depend—i.e. jobs, other people's opinions, money, status. A loss of a job will no longer result in that feeling of nakedness, or cause us to believe that we've lost a piece of ourselves.

When we nurture our 'why's' we begin to cultivate a different foundation that is far sturdier than the ups and downs of a job.

In that state, a job loss can actually serve as a golden opportunity for us to reinvent ourselves.

These are 8 additional myths about job losses which create the wrong stories in our heads and thwart our efforts to go to new levels.

#1 *You are radioactive material to be shunned.* It is very true that many people, even former colleagues, may not be sure how to interact with you if you've been fired, or have left your job in a cloud of conflict with your employer. Typically, others will have received only a portion of the story, or will have their own opinions about why you left—right or wrong, fair or unfair. As such, they may avoid communication with you, or simply leave future interactions to chance. For most people, this behavior will have no malice attached to it—they may simply not know how to get beyond the awkwardness. Show them grace and move on. Whether people avoid contact with you, or decide to reach out to you on LinkedIn, don't put too much emphasis on either response to your departure. Focus forward and ignore opinions.

#2 *Your job history is in peril.* Once you leave a job, you should immediately update your list of references. If you've been able to plan your exit strategy, you should have this list updated well before you re-enter the workforce. If your departure was more sudden, leaving you little to no time to secure a reference from your manager—or unsure if you'd even receive one—there are always other options. You can reach into the network which you've built across your career, and find people who can speak to your skills, experience and leadership style. Perhaps those were peers at your prior company, or even direct reports. Build the list and reach out to them. Your manager's reference is certainly desirable, but no single person has that much control over your future—so don't sweat it should your prior manager disappear as an option.

#3 *You need to bury the truth about your job loss.* Bestselling author, Ann Aguirre, wrote that "once exposed, a secret loses all its power." You own everything that happened to you—good, bad and in between. Obviously, we must all use good judgment and wisdom in deciding what to share, and with whom, depending upon the circumstances. In the more difficult situations with an employer, the journey towards 'what's next' starts with leaning in to your job loss. Remember, you have not lost yourself. As Nancy Karas shared, we need to operate more like CEOs of our own careers. Secondly, writing your comeback story is part of your own personal reinvention. You now get to give others a window into that reinvention. (I share more on personal reinventions in Chapter 9.) Work on packaging the core events of your departure in ways that capture three vital components: truth about the change; learnings about yourself and your former employer; and confidence about your value and future. Don't bury the truth without giving it one *heck'uva* send-off as you get it behind you. Share your story, tout your credentials then pivot to your 'what's next.'

#4 *A handful of people have a monopoly on the best jobs.* If you haven't networked heavily in some time, you may naturally think that the best opportunities are reserved only for the fortunate few. Great job opportunities have a way of getting to the right people at the right times. This is why it's so important to continually build and nurture your professional network. Active network engagement creates multiple touchpoints to individuals who can provide support or offer advice when you most need it. That support and advice will often lead to new contacts which can, ultimately, open new doors.

#5 *You must spend all of your time job hunting.* When you're back out in the job market, you'll naturally experience a degree of anxiety, particularly if your transition is unanticipated. One of the ways that anxiety will manifest itself is through a daily addiction to your computer—as you feel compelled to cling to every job board posting and potential source of employment. However, the right opportunity will be surfaced through the quality of your search, not the quantity. In fact, spending all of your time applying to jobs, or following up on leads can actually result in diminishing returns. You'll need to be much more strategic. It's better to take the time to (re)create your professional roadmap, then identify the various opportunities, organizations or entrepreneurial pursuits that make sense for you at this stage. Beyond the need to be strategic, you'll need to be re-energized and refocused. Following up on those doctor's appointments which you could never make time for, catching up on the books in your reading queue, and generally being good to yourself—whatever that means to you—is more important than ever during this period.

#6 *You are too old to make a shift in your career.* As long as you have the strength, drive, and clarity of vision about your career—you will never be too old to make a change! But, there is an unspoken truth about the professional marketplace: ageism exists. This is particularly true for women—as the workplace is simply a microcosm of a larger societal bias against female aging. Aside from the gender factor, older workers face an outdated notion that they lack the energy of their younger counterparts—even though today's older workers are far more active and healthier than in years past. It is also often wrongly assumed that they are lagging behind technologically. So, there are real huddles to jump during a job transition as an older worker. But, for every hurdle, there is an equal or greater opportunity to be seized. With age comes wisdom and insights which you can apply in a variety of settings. Now is the time to reflect on successful roles or volunteer projects from your past experiences. What did you enjoy most about that work? What skills did you employ? Perhaps you can take a continuing education course to refine and build upon those skills. There's no time like the present. Don't allow today's negative thoughts to rob you of tomorrow's successes. (I share more about ageism in Chapter 8.)

#7 *You are too young to make a shift in your career.* There is still a presumed conventional wisdom which suggests that you must "pay your dues" once entering a particular field, before making a shift into a new one. You may even receive advice urging you to stick it out if you become severely uninspired by your current profession and are tempted to initiate the change yourself. If you take this advice, you may eventually discover after a decade or more, that you hate your job, no longer have a clear sense of direction, and generally feel uninspired. You are not too young to make a shift, and there are no rules-of-thumb that should dictate your mobility, ambition, or motivations—as long as you are honest and studious about your career moves. If you've been fired from your job, it may very well be the biggest blessing at this stage in your career. For young women in particular, career advancement must be carefully plotted to avoid falling into ruts. Be careful to strike a careful balance along the way—before, during, and after any career shifts—between taking on more work to increase your visibility, and not being afraid to say 'no' when your workload becomes out of balance. The sooner you develop this balanced approach, the more confident you'll become when making any shifts in your budding career.

#8 *You must jump on the first job offer that comes along.* Rather than buy into that notion, think of yourself as a unique talent who will add value wherever you go. Doesn't your uniqueness require careful consideration of all options? You need to ensure that you'll be a good fit, not only for the position, but for the culture of the new company. You may want to challenge the compensation package being offered in order to avoid settling for something that would place an undue strain on your pocketbook down the road. Finally, you may just need to decline the offer altogether if you believe deeply in the pursuit of a completely new path. Saying 'yes' now may provide temporary security, but it could also result in a missed future opportunity to take your career—and your life—to new heights.

Benefits of Failure

Giving ourselves permission to miss the mark at times, is vital to our growth and development. Whether or not we grant ourselves that permission, missing the mark will happen anyway—so we might as well prepare for it. In fact, when we experience failure, we should view it as an opportunity to be strategically leveraged. It contains several benefits.

- It provides clarity to our situations, forcing us to zoom in on the most important things.
- It frees us from the chokeholds of false, self-created narratives suggesting that we have it all figured out, and that we're perfect.
- It forces us to be more creative. Failure is, essentially, the elimination of a bad option. After failing, we're more motivated to devise better options—this time with more experience and more information.
- It tells us who our true friends/colleagues are. Those who scatter during times of failure show us who they are, and we should believe them (*adaptation from Maya Angelou's quote*).
- It creates a spirit of resilience. Perhaps a job loss will represent one of your most dreaded fears. After it occurs, you can then say "I've been there, done that, and got the T-shirt!" You will have learned, course-corrected, and can now return better than before.

This doesn't just apply to losing one's job—it can apply to other types of losses. In July of 2018, American tennis star, Serena Williams, used her platform to help women—and men— around the world understand how to benefit from failure. She battled back to the Wimbledon finals after a near death experience during childbirth, and several fits and starts once she returned to the game of tennis. She struggled to achieve the balance between being a new wife and mother, and playing the game of tennis that catapulted her to amazing success. Though she lost the game in July at that Wimbledon match, she won the hearts and minds of women—especially mothers—around the world. She used the loss of that particular game to talk about determination, and to express the importance of resilience...she let the world know that one loss did not define her journey.

If you happen to lose your job, you still have *you*—and that's worth a whole lot.

You'll never build your character, or reap the benefits which I've described above if you're holding on too tightly to the reality of what was, or the notion of what could have been. Disappointments, failures, and major transitions hold the keys to new beginnings.

Tough As Nails · Big Ideas

✓ You and your job *are* mutually exclusive

✓ Give yourself the gift of acknowledging your emotions through the period of a job loss. You may bend through this challenge, but you won't break

✓ Not all job losses are created equal—your emotions, recovery and next steps will differ with each type of loss (pgs. 93-96)

✓ In order to successfully secure an identity which is separate from a job, you must understand your 'why's' in life

✓ A job loss can be a golden opportunity to reinvent yourself

✓ Become familiar with the other 8 myths about job losses, as they can thwart your efforts to go to new levels (pgs. 96-102)

✓ We must give ourselves permission to fail in order to reap the benefits (pg. 102-103)

✓ Disappointments, failures, and major transitions hold the keys to new beginnings

Pearls from Jo's Journal

I think we're all guilty of allowing other people, and circumstances, to have an undue amount of control or influence over our careers. Our lives are made up of a million moments. No one moment is the end-all, or be-all of our entire existence. We have the ability to change our circumstances. This doesn't mean it will be easy. We may need to cry some tears, conquer some fears, and age some years—but it's a necessary part of our journeys. I think that the times when we least expect to have to make a major change, are precisely the times when we need to.

Chapter 8

Race and Age Factors

Finding your voice in the workplace as a woman is complicated. I'm certain that what you've read thus far in this book has only cemented your awareness of that fact. Today, the number of women around any given conference room table across companies may have risen, but many of the sabotaging behaviors which I described in Chapter 1 are slow to disappear. However, I'm pleased to say that I've personally grown more comfortable pushing back on this behavior, using my authentic voice to take my rightful place around *any* given table. I've also learned to be strategic about when and how I decide to push back. And, moreover, I do so without the slightest degree of vitriol against my awesome brothers.

In addition to being a woman, I'm also black and have more than 25 years in business. All three of these categories represent an important part of my personal and professional journey. Unfortunately, the workplace can, at times, be quite hostile to those who bring these additional distinctions to the table. I don't share this as a statement of victimhood. I never have and never will. However, my differences have been an undeniable part of my experience and demand thoughtful reflection.

The Race Factor

Being black in the workplace brings unique challenges. Seeking to understand these challenges creates the pathway to learning opportunities. It's a complicated pathway, largely because many people are reticent to have the uncomfortable conversations surrounding issues of race. However, it's those very conversations which give all those willing to engage, fresh perspectives and vital revelations which result in healthier workplaces.

In my own experience, I've lost count of the number of people—outside of my own race—who have asked me where I grew up, minutes into our first conversation. While the question itself may appear benign, it has always been about the timing and tone of the inquiry with which I take issue. The question tends to reveal an assumption often made about well-spoken black people: that we grew up in more privileged (a.k.a. white) environments. This is a complex subject to tackle in a few lines of a book. Suffice it to say that, while justifications may sometimes exist for these assumptions, it is never okay to hold lower expectations of an individual because of their race or ethnicity—even when the end result is complimentary.

As a black woman in the workplace, I have a built-in impulse to defend other people of color when I sense any disparagement toward them. This disparagement is not always rooted in deep seated racism. Oftentimes, it can be born out of cultural ignorance.

I was once in a meeting where a white male cracked a joke about a black woman's natural hairstyle. I believe the comment was innocently foolish, though laced with a bias toward what is considered a 'normal' hairstyle in the workplace. The ensuing conversations and fence-mending after that particular episode were, and still are, rich lessons in diversity and inclusion. I'm hopeful that it taught all those involved the sort of sensitivity needed in how we communicate with each other, and the strengthening effect on an organization with members willing to call out the wrong behavior.

I recently spoke with an inspiring leader and woman of color, as I sought to glean additional insights into this sensitive topic of race in the workplace. Tequilla Brownie, Ed.D., is an Executive Vice President at The New Teacher Project (TNTP) and Chair of TNTP's Diversity Leadership Council (*TNTP is a national nonprofit founded by teachers working to help school systems end educational inequality and achieve their goals for students*).

As Tequilla shared the intricacies of her journey, I was endeared to a place—work or otherwise—where we could be truly blind to color, and any other differences. In this place, we would operate with only our human vulnerabilities as the common thread that binds us together.

With refreshing candor, Tequilla peeled away the veneer around what it means to be both black and a woman in today's workplace. She said that "it's difficult to wear the cloak of womanhood, blackness, and leadership all within the same wardrobe. If I'm honest, I would much prefer to leave one of the garments in the closet for just one day. But the truth of the matter is that I can't. I won't. For better or for worse, the essence of me includes being a woman, being black, and being a senior leader in a predominately white workplace." Tequilla shared how much love she has for her career and organization, yet admitted that those facts don't "diminish the weight of the garments" that travel with her every day.

Tequilla's description of that nagging sense that, as women leaders of color, we must be preoccupied with demonstrating our worth and worthiness—resonated powerfully with me. This preoccupation, as she shared, invites a "burden." It is the type of burden that can cause many of us to embrace a "stage persona to exemplify a confidence" which masks our true feelings. Without a doubt, many of these burdens have roots in the uglier periods of our great nation's history. Nevertheless, they are not insurmountable. So, how do we overcome them using our authentic voices?

One way is to be intentional about how we show up to the workplace. Tequilla describes this as "choosing our own narratives." That narrative requires an ability to be both authentic and astute about our workplace surroundings. Many of us practice regular self-reflection in our efforts to strike these delicate balances. Tequilla shared that "daily, I ask myself questions about how I want to be perceived, and what I want people to know about me, my strengths, and development areas."

Another one of her strategies in navigating the complexities of leading as a woman of color, is to remind herself of the enormous value that she brings to the workplace. Tequilla says that, "I'm well aware that I'm not perfect...but, I've worked to become more familiar and honest with myself about my own strengths and my own assets. This means that I'm able to show up in a way that maximizes those things that I'm good at." This, as Tequilla reveals, helps her "feel more moments of success vs.

failure" which can provide her with that needed boost of self-confidence.

I personally want what Tequilla wants: "to feel whole and able to leverage the assets and perspectives that enhance my work, because of—not in spite of—the fact that I am a Black woman."

Tequilla's final point speaks to the importance of personal and professional circles of supporters. Women of color—and all women—need people around us who will operate as "sisters, mothers, cheerleaders, critical friends and coaches."

Race is an important dimension of finding your voice in the workplace among the diversity of people, personalities and backgrounds. We all approach this exercise to understand and interpret the race dynamic very differently. Yet, all of the strategies which Tequilla described can be applied to every demographic in the workplace. And, that may be the most important takeaway: we are different, and, in so many ways—we are all the same. Both of those realizations must be acknowledged and celebrated.

Ultimately, the goal is to ensure that we have the honest conversations needed to help women and men, across all races and ethnicities, find—and keep—their authentic voices within an ever-changing business environment.

The Age Factor

I am one among the shrinking population of Generation X-ers in the workplace. I often feel under-appreciated for the unique perspectives which I offer in any setting. While the experts scramble to publish the next insightful article on the Millennial takeover of the workplace and the need to understand that generation, I am a female, seasoned worker who would benefit from the same level of analysis. I can share myriad experiences in a variety of companies where I worked, with great tenacity, through the issues challenging today's businesses. I, like my Millennial brothers and sisters, have an entrepreneurial spirit and a deep desire to disrupt things in a quest for something new and better.

And, I'm certainly not alone. Seasoned workers are, at once, ambitious, optimistic, savvy about change, and achievement-oriented—all characteristics which describe the Millennial generation. High performers are not segmented by generational categories. Workers with decades of experience understand the urgency of the moment, the need for agility, and the importance of leading among competitors. Many of us know all too well, the fates that met the companies who failed to understand this need for speed and innovation. We may have even worked at those companies whose biographies are now reserved for case studies at universities imparting wisdom on how *not* to run a business. So, employers would be wise to be more intentional about engaging and fully leveraging seasoned workers.

A failure to tap into the richness of experiences found among more seasoned workers, also causes their age to fall victim to stigmatization. Finding one's voice and place in the work environment is hard enough. When that voice is attached to a woman who is traversing an uneven landscape, the stigma of age becomes yet another barrier making progress exponentially harder.

To highlight this point, below, I include another real-life example from Jo Weech. Jo is the Founder and Principal Consultant of Exemplary Consultants, which assists startups and small companies in the areas of People, Talent and Operations. Jo is a sought-after conference speaker, who shares her strategies, successes, and failures on topics including employee engagement, recruiting, and diversity and inclusion. She is a leader who has been quite vocal about ageism in the workplace. Jo recently wrote a LinkedIn article[12] about her experiences with ageism which, in just a few weeks, was read by over 172,000 people, and received thousands of responses from people across six different continents.

The stigmatization of age—a woman's age, in particular—often occurs in stealthy and cryptic ways.

In Jo's case, she was confronted with this issue after her role as Chief People Officer for a software engineering startup was eliminated. It was at that point that Jo believed that "the entire landscape had changed." The Age Discrimination in Employment Act of 1967 (ADEA) was somehow failing in its promise to protect older workers from discrimination. Throughout her job search, Jo found that the reasons given to her for why she was not selected for a particular role, revealed far more than a tinge of ageism. It was after a year of these disappointing conversations that she decided to pen her pivotal LinkedIn article intended to shed light on the issue.

The responses to her article revealed story after story of readers' experiences with the same issue. In being bold enough to confront this problem, Jo helped many individuals and employers to move toward lasting solutions.

One solution which Jo espouses, is to challenge women to continue to walk what she describes as that "fine line between being authentic and real" as we call out areas of bias, without the fear of being labelled negatively. When we are willing to confront those issues, and to do the homework required to influence our audiences to make decisions in our favor—we are one step closer to winning this battle. Jo said it best: "We mustn't fear. We need to stand tall and be confident in all that we are and what we can do. But, we do not get to bulldoze our way to the 'table.' We must let data do the talking. We should arm ourselves with data analytics for anything we wish to accomplish; let the data be our voice. Data can be leveraged to tell a story that might not be heard otherwise, no matter how compelling our presentation."

Jo also shared an inspiring story of how she used her voice to effect change "one person at a time." Once, as she was applying for a job, she noticed the company's Applicant Tracking System required college graduation dates from its applicants, even before their resume could be submitted for consideration. So, what did Jo do? She sent the company's representatives an email and raised a red flag, letting them know that this approach could easily be used to discriminate against candidates on the basis of age. When they bristled, she pushed back on behalf of applicants everywhere. To the company's credit, they later disabled this particular feature of the system.

Using your voice in the workplace could result in making a difference far beyond your personal circumstance. This requires being concerned about the broader issues which can sometimes negatively impact our sisters and brothers around the globe. As

Jo shared, you can effect change "by speaking up, without 'attitude', but with confidence in the rightness of your position." Amen!

Tough As Nails · Big Ideas

✓ Race and age factors are an important and undeniable part of the workplace experience

✓ Courageous conversations about race issues serve to catalyze fresh perspectives which, in turn, result in healthier workplaces

✓ Women of color can "choose our own narratives", remind ourselves—daily—of our strengths, and surround ourselves with a circle of supporters

✓ Workers with decades of experience are best positioned to understand the many nuances of a dynamic business environment

✓ High performers are not segmented by generational categories

✓ Using your voice in the workplace could result in making a difference far beyond your personal circumstance

Pearls from Jo's Journal

During these latter stages of my career, I've actually relished the opportunities to have courageous conversations about race issues, in particular, in the workplace. I've secretly enjoyed watching the look on someone's face who is absolutely shocked when I raise what they may consider a taboo topic about race. After the shock passes, the next reaction is often relief, followed by a visible sense of freedom to be more honest about their thoughts on the matter. That's what we need. Honesty. As long as we share what's on our minds with respect, we can learn so much from each other. When that happens, the entire workplace wins.

Chapter 9

Reinventing Yourself

At some point in your career as a woman aspiring to do great things in your corner of the world, you may experience a period in which you will need—or want—to reinvent yourself.

In Chapter 7, I shared practical advice for navigating your way through situations which resulted in the loss of your employment. While the loss of a job can be a stressful and disorienting period, it can also present one of the most transformative opportunities to go to new levels. Personal reinvention is often born out of a crucible moment in one's life, where an original path has become muddied or has disappeared as an option altogether.

What can you do when change creates a series of choices? You can choose. Women are often at the center of conversations surrounding choices: a choice to leave the workforce to have a child; a choice to delay their return to the workforce after the birth of a child; the choice to be a stay-at-home mother; the choice to strike their own unique version of work/life balance, etc. You will also have the choice to take control of the diverse options laid before you. Perhaps you may be stirred to reinvent your entire career landscape, and find an entirely new professional footing.

Whether that moment of choice comes naturally or unnaturally, you will need to be thoughtful about your reinvention journey. Enter the first leg of that journey, then keep traveling to arrive at what may be an unanticipated destination. There are key actions and considerations which can serve as a light to guide you along the way.

Operating at the Crossroads

There are things in our lives which, if we're honest, we would admit may not be materializing the way we had envisioned. Those things run the full gamut of life. Changes at work, or in our professions, may place us at a pivotal crossroad—forcing us to make tough decisions about our 'what's next.'

If you're in this period of major transition, what you choose next will either cement your current career path, change it slightly, or alter it dramatically. The key question to ask yourself during this period is—how much discomfort and risk are you willing to tolerate? Circumstances surrounding your household income, savings, and people who may depend on you will clearly be included in your calculus. The balance between familiarity and risk comes down to your willingness to embrace the unknown.

At times, the crossroad may be thrust upon you through a job loss as I've shared. In those circumstances, you can use the energy from that imposed crossroad to propel you forward rather than waste it on self-defeating thoughts, or allow inertia to take hold. Take comfort in the fact that you will always have data from which to draw as you make key decisions. This data has come consciously and unconsciously from the library of your life experiences. Oftentimes, as women, we are quick to look at other women whom we admire and wonder what they would do in our situations. However, every situation is different, because the people and details involved are different. When you arrive at a crossroad in your professional life, be sure to draw from your own database rather than let the amount of energy and years which you've spent accumulating it, go to waste.

Stick to the Essentials

On any given day of any given week, we are too often overwhelmed. We are perpetually overcommitted. We have many times overpromised something to someone, and are living with the fear of under-delivering. When we are at the precipice of reinventing ourselves, the last thing we need is clutter in our lives. In Chapter 3, I shared the importance of exerting the power that each of us holds over how we spend our time. Being busy does not equate to productivity. At your crossroad moment, you will need to say 'no,' more, in order to get to the right 'yes.' You will need to carefully assess how you've been spending your time to ensure that your activities are serving you, rather than sapping you of precious time and energy. That includes volunteer activities, professional associations, relationships, and bad habits (i.e. overeating, too much TV binge watching—*ouch*). Make a list of the likely clutter targets and go over them, one by one, until your justifications for holding onto them begin to wane.

Engage Your Truthteller

There is a point in our lives, particularly as women, when we must be intentional about caring for ourselves in order to take the next big step forward. Many of us are not great at self-care, as we've settled into the role of caring for everyone—and everything—else. When we're confronted with the need to change, we will periodically need to reduce our giving tendencies in order to avoid the depletion of our emotional, and other, resources. Only then can we learn, or rediscover, how to truly listen for the truth about our situations. That truth may take any number of forms. It could be the truth about a job that we hate, but settled for; or the truth about our fear of change; or the truth about our inability to develop new skills and accept feedback. The truth is hard to hear even when one *is* listening.

There are many truths along a professional path that, in order to surface, will require becoming vulnerable. You'll need the help of a truthteller. This person could be your spouse, friend, or another family member. However, the right professional coach is more likely the type of objective source you'll need to dissect and reconstruct the most pertinent issues at your reinvention crossroad.

The right coach can breathe clarity into those hazy periods in your life, and help you to devise sound strategies which can break through the fog. Rather than flying blind into the wilderness, a coach can help you check your motives, clarify your desires, and arm you with tools to take a particular strategy to fruition. There are many people quite skilled at this. The trick is to look for someone with the skill *and* passion for this work, and one who meshes with your personality.

Dream Big, With Deadlines

Life is entirely too short to slide from day to day with no clear sense of direction. This kind of living can easily creep into your professional life unless, and until, you are jolted by a crossroad moment. Those moments will be the engine of your personal and professional reinvention. Those moments can also serve to resurrect dreams buried long ago.

> **During this period of reinvention, you may have the opportunity to live up to those dreams, rather than just living up to your income.**

The longer-term picture will become more important to you as opposed to the daily ruts which you may have fallen into. When you dust off those dreams, be sure to polish them with specifics. As you work through the next leg of your professional journey, perhaps with the help of a coach, break your dream down into bite-sized pieces and manageable parts. Define actions and milestones, right down to the steps required to be taken today. Now may be the time to replace blind loyalty to a company, with a steadfast loyalty to your own long-term economic, physical, and spiritual health.

Accept Your Imperfections

The amount of time which we all spend pretending to have it altogether, is simply a futile effort to hide the fact that we're all flawed. There are volumes of literature written about the reasons for why we choose to torture ourselves with quests for perfection: childhood experiences, bad bosses, a teacher's influence. The list to explain how we tend to wrestle with the desire for perfection is also endless.

Women, as I've shared, have a unique struggle with this desire. In a 2009 study published in The Journal of Occupational and Organizational Psychology, the researchers found that women are more likely than men to feel a sense of failing to meet their own standards around work and family commitments. Two issues seem evident here: 1) self-imposed standards set by women are likely herculean, and 2) the effort expended in striving to meet those standards is creating a self-defeating cycle of despair. Perfectionism is an unworthy and damaging goal (I share more about my own experiences in Chapter 10).

When you've entered a crossroad in your professional life, you will need to embrace this lesson more than ever. If you don't, you may be choosing a path towards anxiety, depression, eating disorders, and other ills. Recognizing the inevitability and importance of imperfection, will free you to experiment. In that more realistic world, failure will be a reasonable option.

Experimentation is a great friend during this period of reinvention. Exploring new opportunities is like trying on a few amazing dresses until you get to just the right style and the right size. The dress may not have even fit several years ago. In fact, you may have hated that style at some point. But, now, not only does the dress fit—it maximizes your very best features and minimizes the rest.

Take Stock of—and Celebrate—Your Journey

Operating at a professional crossroad is mentally exhausting. It can be quite disorienting. It calls into question everything you thought you knew about yourself—forcing you to reconstruct those truths, or cast them aside entirely. For those of you who take great comfort in stability and are loath to step into uncharted territory, your reinvention journey is worth deep reflection—and great celebration. You have conquered, or are coming face-to-face with that giant called 'fear.'

Along this journey, you'll need to be deliberate in looking back to see just how far you've come. Celebrate the baby steps as well as the major milestones. If you've worked up the nerve to contact a complete stranger to ask for what turned out to be pivotal advice—celebrate it. If you've just accepted a speaking engagement that will, for the first time, place you in front of hundreds of people—celebrate it. If you've been bold enough to say 'no' to what others have told you would be the best opportunity you'd be able to get during your transitional period—celebrate it. Celebrate it all. You'll be amazed and proud of how far you've come as you take stock of these moments.

When Making Decisions

Crossroad moments demand that you exercise a higher level of decision-making. The choice between what to order for lunch can be left to a coin flip. However, making a life-changing decision about a shift in career that means you and your family will have to move to another city, requires a more structured thought process. While there are many methodologies available on how to make sound decisions related to business issues, the advice on how to effectively make decisions with a more personal impact, tends to be more scattershot. But, there are ways to structure your thinking and tactics during this latter stage of your reinvention journey.

- When faced with choices, take the time to wrestle with your least favorite—or your most risky—option. If there are big changes to be made in your life, you must expect some degree of tension or discomfort. The road to reinvention may have multiple crossroads. You may be weighing the benefits of taking a step backward in your current career in order to prepare you for a leap forward in another. Or, your next step may be to return to school after having left the educational setting two decades ago. Whatever the choices in front of you, dance with the one you feel is the least attractive. Bounce it off those who know you well, and those who know very little about you. The point here is to take the most honest approach to exploring a variety of perspectives.

- Beware of the 'confirmation bias' trap. Over the course of our lifetimes we have developed a series of beliefs which, if challenged, can make us defensive or simply uncomfortable. We will work unconsciously to confirm those beliefs or ideas that are familiar and closely held— seeking out or accepting information that conforms neatly to them. Reinventing ourselves, by definition, means creating something new or different. An increased awareness of our tendency to confirm what we already believe, is the first step in avoiding this trap.

- Don't convince yourself that more information is necessarily better. While obtaining a variety of perspectives is important, too much data can cause the brain to, quite literally, shut down. When there is simply too much to choose from, the area in the brain responsible for decision-making becomes overwhelmed and can no longer be depended upon to make smart decisions.[13] It is, therefore, vital to limit the amount of data and to apply more rigor to your decision-making process.

• Don't think that making charts and lists are just for college classes. Narrowing your choices as you move toward life-altering decisions can include some science. Decision-making can be greatly facilitated by establishing more order to the process. You can use a spreadsheet that can be as simple, or as complicated as you'd like. It will help to isolate pros, cons, and rankings of the options which you're assessing along your reinvention path.

When all is said and done, the above actions could result in an independent career as a budding entrepreneur. Or, they may lead you to spread your new wings within a company that allows you to bring more of your gifts and talents to the table. Either way, you are poised for the next phase of your journey in a way that may never present itself again.

On Entrepreneurship

If you were writing a letter to your younger self, is it possible that part of your advice might be to seriously consider becoming an entrepreneur? Now that you've thoughtfully reflected on the opportunities to reinvent yourself, entrepreneurship may very well be your landing place. You may discover that—in addition to your technical or functional skills—you have many of the traits of entrepreneurs: innovative; motivated by challenges; tendency to lead, and action orientation; resourceful; intense curiosity; and extreme dissatisfaction with the status quo.

As you embark upon this venture, remember this: as an entrepreneur, your first valuation calculated should be your self-worth, not your net worth. You should be at a point in your life where your personal sense of validation can be drawn from your own reservoir, as opposed to external sources. That confidence will allow you to put your toe in the water with a new concept or product as an entrepreneur, and to become increasingly comfortable with any failures along the way.

Building your self-worth means taking an account of your successes, strengths, attributes, and potential. It also means operating in that place of authenticity. You can't climb to new heights in someone else's shoes. You must be yourself. Hold onto that special sauce of yours that I described in Chapter 1. Conforming to another person's view of how you should dress, what you should sound like, and any other identifying characteristics is a sure path to killing your authenticity. In a competitive business environment, your greatest asset is the uniqueness which you bring to the table. Revealing your authentic self to prospective clients will make it infinitely easier to package your skills, talents, and overall abilities—which is particularly important during a period of reinvention.

'Packaging' yourself through a 30-second elevator pitch is a concept whose importance can never be overstated. Our individual presentations to others must be delivered with the perfect pitch, and be tailored to the situation. You'll need to take the time to work on that soundbite of who you are and what you'd like others to know about you. This will ensure that, whether you're riding an elevator with a potential contact, or simply writing a note to a LinkedIn connection—you can describe yourself in the most compelling manner possible. That description should include: who you are; what you do; and what you have to offer. It should be precise, yet it should leave the listener or reader wanting more. Practice this on trusted members of your inner circle and invite their honest feedback.

As you build new contacts and expand your network, give yourself permission to be bold about asking for what you want and need, without the fear of rejection. As an entrepreneur you can expect many 'no's' before you get to a 'yes' from someone who is interested in what you have to offer. The rejection will build your perseverance and resilience, both of which are traits greatly needed on an entrepreneurial journey.

You should always be intentional about how much you're willing to give away as you build your business. Many people will seek help from you, ask you for favors, or request some of your resources for free. Strike a good balance among using those interactions to increase your contacts; supporting colleagues along their own journeys—and spending your time and energies judiciously. At some point—hopefully sooner rather than later—you'll need to get paid for your services and brainpower. For example, if someone is looking to establish a program that happens to be your area of specialization as a budding entrepreneur, and they ask you for help and guidance—give it to them. However, if they return to the well for more water, give them your hourly rate or flat fee so that they understand the true value of your offerings.

On Intrapreneurship

Who can be described as an intrapreneur? She is one who is bent on innovating within a company, with the tenacity to pursue better ideas and smarter solutions. Instead of establishing her own venture, an intrapreneur works on the inside of a company with the same desire to transform and elevate that particular business.

Your reinvention journey may affirm your belief that you are better suited in someone else's office as opposed to paying the bills for your own office setup. If this is the case, you'll want to work for an employer and within a culture that gives you the space to flourish and to do your best work for them.

The next move in your intrapreneurial journey will be pivotal. You should establish certain non-negotiables in order to avoid massive disappointments or derailments. Perhaps your new company knows how to integrate a 'start-up' environment within their current organizational structure. Or, they will understand how to provide you with assignments that stretch your thinking, present tremendous learning opportunities, and are devoid of the typical bureaucratic barriers. Make a list of those non-negotiables so that you're able to make an informed decision when the next offer comes your way.

Whatever path you choose, your reinvention will be a wonderful milestone in your life. And, it will likely surface some things that you've either not dealt with up to that point, or things that you've not dealt with honestly. Now is your time. Take full advantage of it.

Tough As Nails · Big Ideas

✓ Personal reinvention is often born out of a crucible moment in one's life

✓ The key question during a period of major transition is: how much discomfort and risk are you willing to tolerate?

✓ When you arrive at a crossroad in your professional life, draw from the data accumulated from your life experiences when making tough decisions

✓ At your crossroad moment, you'll need to say 'no' more, to get to the right 'yes'

✓ The right professional coach can help you to dissect, and reconstruct, the most pertinent issues at your reinvention crossroad

✓ Dust off your dreams, then break them down into bite-sized pieces

✓ Recognizing the inevitability and importance of your imperfections, will free you to experiment

✓ Be deliberate about celebrating both the baby steps and major milestones of your reinvention journey

✓ Crossroad moments demand higher level decision-making processes (pgs. 125-127)

✓ Your reinvention journey could result in a career as a budding entrepreneur, or as an intrapreneur in the right company (pgs. 127-130)

Pearls from Jo's Journal

The decision to write this book is part of my own personal reinvention. I've always been a very private person. Deep reflections about the impact of childhood experiences weren't meant to be shared outside of my family circle—or so I thought. The process of writing a book has been difficult. Yet, it has been a wonderfully eye-opening new phase of my personal and professional journey. It has helped me to put decades of living, and a lengthy career, into sharper perspective. I've always toyed with the idea of writing a book, but the timing of that endeavor was never quite as clear as it is now. Today, I understand more fully that my personal and professional experiences were not just intended to make me stronger and wiser—but to help others. In my view, that's really the point of one's reinvention journey: to navigate your way through challenges and opportunities, to bring others along, and to share key lessons with them. *#BetterTogether*

Chapter 10

Embrace the BOSS in You!

This final Chapter has special significance to me. It symbolizes the culmination of what has been a long and winding road to finding my own authentic voice in the workplace.

You'll remember from what I shared in earlier Chapters, that I spent years struggling with insecurities and fears about what others would think about me. These fears began at my earliest and most foundational years.

I have always been studious with a love for the English language. I remember one day bringing home my graded English quiz to show my parents. My mother took one look at the mark-ups on the paper, and immediately questioned the teacher's assessment. She felt so strongly about it that she wrote directly to the teacher and gave him a written tongue-lashing. The next day, that teacher—perhaps unwittingly—did more to submerge my burgeoning sense of confidence than any other teacher over the next several years. He retaliated against my mother and her criticisms by embarrassing me—having me review my answers in front of the class, then highlighting my errors. It was humiliating. Decades later, I still remember how it made me feel.

After that, I returned to the habit of worrying about everything. I spent quite a bit of time alone—free from prying eyes which I believed were judging my every look, my every move. I was on an emotionally exhausting and futile expedition towards perfection. As an extreme introvert, I internalized many things which would have been better processed through dialogue and interaction with others. The exercise of gleaning feedback and making any adjustments was too painful for me. So, I avoided any situation which could reveal my ignorance on any matter.

As I grew older, I had a new monster to slay as I fretted daily about my body image. By then, I'd learned to suffer in silence. Expressing myself through clothes, different colors and the use of accessories felt off limits to me at the time. Black and gray colors became the favored wardrobe choices during my twenties.

My love of the English language kept me hungry for expression. I wrote poems and read voraciously. But, early on in my career, I was still not comfortable with my voice, figuratively speaking. As for my literal voice, I still had the scars from childhood of being teased mercilessly about the tone and tenor of it. The kids in school had convinced me that I sounded like a man. By now, I was at the early stages of my career and was in roles which required presenting to others. Talking was, needless to say, non-negotiable in the workplace.

This period was akin to a butterfly bursting forth from its cocoon. I was steadily becoming more comfortable with myself. I graduated from dealing with violently shaking hands during meetings, to adding a comment or two during the discussions.

Eventually, I was asked to take on other assignments which thrust me into stand-up training and workshop facilitation. I still remember becoming queasy just before I had to speak or lead a session. Each of those moments was a stepping stone to the next. Before long, I realized just how much I loved speaking. I actually enjoyed facilitating meetings. I relished the opportunity to impart information and concepts to others.

As I moved through my career, I began to use my voice in small groups and in larger, public settings. I honed this skill and began to view it as an art. I bought books on the topic. I practiced in front of the mirror. I've always had a good memory, so I was able to absorb large swaths of information and regurgitate it on demand. This became quite useful during speeches or presentations. My love of words propelled me to use them more boldly.

As I was maturing as a professional in business, I was also maturing outside of the workplace. I was now married and starting to have children. As one who spent so much time in silence and who struggled to find myself, and my voice— becoming a mother was a strange experience in more ways than one. Anyone with children understands that there are times when you must switch from the 'sweet mommy'—to the 'no-nonsense-take-charge mommy'. This requires using your voice more strongly, and more assertively. The moment when I realized that I didn't have the faintest idea how to do that as a new mother still tickles me to this day. Suddenly, I had this pint-sized human being staring up at me waiting for me to get my act together and tell him what to do...and mean it. I eventually rose to the occasion and had lots of practice with three children.

My overall experiences have made me more sensitive to others who struggle with insecurities and doubts. To this day, if there's someone who appears to be quiet, or seemingly uncomfortable during a business meeting, I make it a point to seek them out and give them the floor. Looking back, I understand why.

Now, at these later stages of my career, I am the one who will spot the fly in the ointment and call it out in the middle of a meeting. Or, if I believe that there's a new way to think about an old issue, I will say so. I'm no longer afraid to express myself. I have been known to speak to the elephant in the room and to raise the so-called 'taboo' topics. I don't do this out of some self-serving need to be elevated. I do it in pursuit of a greater good. I like to problem-solve. I enjoy the hard work of getting to better and smarter solutions. The end game—or ultimate mission—is important to me as I decide where to apply my time and attention.

I've also discovered that there are many people in the workplace who are not always as concerned with the mission. They may be operating under a completely different agenda. Using your voice in the workplace will often mean facing resistance. That resistance may have nothing to do with a serious business issue. Oftentimes, it may simply be foolish bureaucracy at work. Or, it may be a manager who might view you as a competitor instead of an employee to be developed. Unfortunately, people with whom you spend as much as half of your entire day, might turn out to be the biggest impediment to using your voice in the workplace. There are as many reasons for this as there are people and workplaces.

As a woman aspiring to great things, you may find that your creativity and resourcefulness surface the green-eyed monster. And, lest you believe that sexism is always the culprit, I would remind you of Chapter 4 where I tackle the ills of a mean-girl culture. Not everyone will cheer you on when you discover a streamlined way of managing a project, or attempt to bring fresh thinking to team leadership. You may be part of a culture where 'status quo' is the accepted manifesto and any suggestion that it should be altered breeds anger and contempt. For example, if you've joined a company that has yet to embrace a digital work environment, showing up to meetings with your iPad is unlikely to win you any friends—at least not in the early days of your tenure.

So, as you find your voice in the workplace, how exactly—and when—do you use it? The answer is: it depends. It depends on your workplace culture. It depends on the level of support you believe you'll have from the leadership of your company. It depends on your own professional ambitions. And, it depends on you. There are a variety of ways and settings in which you can use your voice successfully. Let's explore a few of them.

The Art of Listening
No one will care if you are using your voice to share information that is off-target or inappropriate. Those around you need to know that you've taken the time to understand their points of view. If you've recently become part of a new workplace culture, the smartest thing you can do is to spend the first few months listening. Resist the urge to jump in with an opinion until you can prove that you have your facts straight. Joining older, more

established brands makes this advice all the more vital, as the legacy issues in those cultures will need to be well understood before your voice will make a bit of difference.

Be Strategic

EF Hutton, the now-defunct American stock brokerage firm, established a motto which became widely known through their commercials: *when EF Hutton talks, people listen.* That should really be the motto of all leaders. You should aspire to be that person who trades the opportunities to add a meager two cents, for the moments where higher impact through more substantive input can be achieved. When you talk, people should listen. If you're talking too much, people will eventually stop listening. Don't feel the need to weigh in on everything. Your commentary could easily become extraneous, which only diminishes your voice when it's most needed.

Take the Temperature

I shared earlier in this Chapter, that I'm now the person to say the thing which is most uncomfortable—to call out that elephant in the room. In addition to being bold enough to speak, I've also learned the importance of reading the room, of taking the pulse of the audience, and studying facial expressions and other body language. This is all integral to taking the temperature before jumping in. If a topic is difficult and you feel that there is still something which must be said, just be careful to pick the time—and even the place—to say it. You may need to prime the pump and hold a pre-conversation with someone outside of the meeting to avoid creating barriers for yourself later on.

Get to the Point

Everyone knows at least one annoying individual who engages in long, rambling monologues in meetings or other settings. I find that women, in particular, tend to share information in shades and layers as opposed to bullet points. Using your voice requires developing the skill of precision. Don't force listeners to sift through extraneous words and phrases to get to the meat of what you're saying. If you're asking a question, ask it. After you raise your question, don't feel the need to fill the quiet spaces or reduce any awkwardness with more words. Get comfortable with the silence after you drop your words of wisdom. That's a powerful sign of confidence.

Disagree Without Leaving an Aftertaste

This is a challenge for many women engaged in a spirited debate or robust dialogue on a heady issue. Too many of us are preoccupied with being liked. There are times when disagreeing with the prevailing opinion may be crucial to moving the dial on a business issue. There is an art to disagreeing. Even when done well, it will still be uncomfortable for many of us. Disagreeing is not the same as being disagreeable. You can share your opinion and make pronouncements which are diametrically opposed to the most powerful person in the room—and do so with class. Avoid language which can be interpreted as confrontational. Use the technique of posing a question to raise a potentially controversial opinion. For example, you can ask a question about a particular business strategy with which you disagree, then offer a variety of alternatives which might enhance the dialogue. If the conversation becomes heated, don't raise your voice. Hold your ground and continue to make your point. It is possible that the rigorous debate could spur a better idea, so relinquish the need to be right. If it becomes clear that the conversation is going nowhere, simply agree to disagree and move on.

Silence the Wrong Voices

Now that you have more tools to use when deciding how and when to use your voice, before using them you may first need to silence those insidious voices in your own head.

Do you feel like a phony? Have you crossed over that line from humility to self-deprecation more often than not? Do you secretly believe that what you've achieved is really no big deal? Are you worried that others around you will reveal how much smarter they are once you engage with them? If you've answered 'yes' to any of these questions, you are likely dealing with what many of us deal with known as the *Impostor Phenomenon or Syndrome*. The term was introduced in 1978 in the article *The Impostor Phenomenon in High Achieving Women: Dynamics and Therapeutic Intervention* by Dr. Pauline R. Clance and Dr. Suzanne A. Imes. Clance and Imes define it as one who experiences a self-perceived intellectual phoniness. While their original findings focused on high-achieving women, additional research has determined that this issue is plaguing just about every demographic and categorization of individuals.[14] In other words, this is another equal opportunity challenge.

Notably, even during the writing of this book—a book designed to help and empower women as they aspire to greater heights—I struggled with a need for perfection. With a richness of experience amassed over decades of my life and career, I still worried whether some of the content would be good enough for public consumption. The good news is that I can celebrate the fact that I now recognize this negative emotion when it rears its ugly head.

I am not perfect, and I'm relieved about that. I must continuously give myself permission to be flawed.

Once that happens, the fall from that fictitious perch has a much softer landing.

The Impostor Syndrome comes in many other forms, yet there are many antidotes which can be deployed to combat it.

One antidote is to accept compliments offered with a genuine sense of gratitude. When someone tells you that you've excelled at a project, or expresses gratitude for what they believe is commendable—pause to say 'thank you.' Don't demur, dismiss the compliment or shift the credit to someone else needlessly. Accept it and take the time to relish in it. When you adopt this as a habit, you will begin to absorb those words of life and encouragement, as you should.

Another way to inhale your own goodness, is to take your time when introducing yourself. I've sat in many meetings where I've heard women in particular, rush through an introduction of themselves and what they do, sometimes choosing to omit their title in that description. I've been guilty of doing the same thing. This is self-defeating behavior. If you're in a meeting or in a setting with people who don't know you, share enough detail to increase their desire to know more. Get used to the sound of your own voice telling the world how awesome you are. I know that this may sound self-serving—but that's the point. You need to think more about yourself, until you reach the place where you're a true believer in your talents and worth.

Another antidote is the science of over-preparation for an important meeting, project or major presentation. I'm not suggesting that you use over preparing as a path to achieve perfection—I've already debunked that myth. However, covering all of your bases and doing your part to ensure that you have complete mastery over whatever the subject matter, will greatly increase your sense of confidence. That kind of confidence will leave little room for doubt and negative thinking.

Your Voice Matters

Ultimately, turning the corner to a place where you believe the headlines on your resume, LinkedIn page, and biography will mean that you are embracing your talents. No longer will you be looking at the gifts of others with envy, but you'll be spending your energy opening up your own.

Finally, all of this should be done in moderation. Recognizing your gifts and talents does not mean always being the first to talk about them, nor does it mean using them to minimize others'. Holding onto a degree of humility will always be important.

As you find and use your voice in the workplace, you will be wise to fully own your professional development. While your employer and immediate manager should of course be interested and invested in your growth—you are the ultimate owner of your career path. Even before we had the benefit of expert guidance and researched-based tools from Gallup, most of us knew that, if given a choice, we'd want to work with people who cared about our own growth and development. There comes a point in our journeys, where sharing our purpose, strengths, areas of development and aspiration is a natural part of our professional lives. It helps to have a manager who is interested in your career, but you may not be as fortunate. We should be cultivating our own development plans once we're clear on our strengths and passions. Either way, you are the primary owner. Develop career plans for the next 6 months, 12 months and 3 years. Along the way, you can ensure that others are providing input into your plan—knowingly or unknowingly—by asking for feedback. Feedback, when received from someone you trust or, at minimum respect, can be a gift. When delivered with compassion, it can be transformative.

It is also important to build a small, professional circle of colleagues who can speak words of wisdom, and inspire you before, during, and after your planning stages.

In your ascent to the top and through any glass ceilings, you may reach a point where you are perfectly positioned for a major leap into, or across, the executive ranks. That positioning may be as an internal candidate in your own company. Just as in other walks of life, people in business can become enthralled with the new or different candidate, often neglecting what they may have right in front of them. When these people are in a position of authority and influence over your candidacy for a position at the next level, you will need to challenge assumptions made about you and fight to be the 'shiny penny' which they're looking for elsewhere.

Of course, any sound interview process will consider an array of candidates and backgrounds. Being an internal candidate is never a guarantee that you're the right person for the role. However, if you believe that you've worked hard to prove yourself, are prepared for the next level, and have bona fide advantages over external candidates—you should reach for that brass ring. If this is you, be sure to: 1) fully understand the search process and embrace it, 2) do your homework leaving no stone unturned, 3) establish a clear and compelling vision and strategy for the role and your first 100 days, if selected, and 4) share the story of your career like someone who is selling something that they believe in. If you're not successful, you will have still won on other fronts. You will have put yourself on the radar of key leaders and stakeholders. You will have undoubtedly learned a lot more about your company and increased your subject matter knowledge. And, you can take the feedback received and apply it to the next opportunity.

YOU are the shiny penny—wherever you go. Walk in that truth as you work to hone your talents and increase your skills. Believing in yourself is the least you can do when others are unwilling to afford you the same.

This reminds me of a meeting that I had many years ago with a senior level recruiter. I'd set up the meeting with her in order to discuss a career transition. At the time, I was still finding my leadership voice, yet I had a persistent sense that I was destined for more. I shared with this recruiter that I wanted to consider applying for C-Suite roles, even the top seat. What I needed from her was that simple nod which leaves the interpretation of emphatic agreement or complete neutrality, up to the receiver. Instead, she actually chuckled and set out to squash my ambitions, redirecting me back to her lower expectations. I felt defeated and yet unconvinced.

I've written this book so that when you are tempted to doubt your greatness, you can sift through the pages written here and find your way again.

I'd like the strongest takeaway from what I've written to be this: YOUR voice matters.

Finding and using it is hard—though not impossible—work. I've been quite deliberate in calling on you to look in the mirror as part of that hard work. We can't speak boldly with our own voices if we don't quiet ourselves to listen intently to the hardest truths. Those truths can come from a variety of sources: our own internal whispers, trusted friends, caring family members, tough bosses, etc. And, sometimes, they can come from a book that falls into the right hands, at the right season in one's life. I hope that this book represents that type of help to you.

Women still have a long road to travel. While it is no longer unheard of for a woman to run a company, or even a large corporation, there are still not enough of us in those positions. One of the best examples of women shattering the oft-discussed glass ceiling, is on the Supreme Court. However, the breakthroughs at more micro levels, still leave much to be desired. Succession planning exercises, where an individual's readiness for the next level is assessed, will forever be lacking if there are not enough women at the start of the pipeline.

Women need to learn from each other. We need to serve as role models by design, and not default. We need to call each other out in constructive ways when our own behavior is at issue. And, importantly, we need to be willing to send the elevator back down when each of us reaches our next level of greatness.

Take the time required to get to the core of who you really are—your authentically awesome self. Develop an assortment of tools to increase your value as you help your company, and the business world at large. Take a long, hard look at how you show up to the workplace and be the first to make the adjustments before expecting anything from others. But, also recognize that the workplace is full of imperfect people—that includes you, me, and all of us. Dysfunction will occur. Company cultures will not always live up to their ideals, but you have the ability to choose—you are the 'CEO of your own career.'

Strive to become the type of leader who is set apart from the rest. Remember that "People don't follow you because you are nice, they follow you because they believe the place you are taking them is better than the place they are [today]." *(Scott Hammerle)*

Being liked as a leader is a nice-to-have. Being respected as a leader is a *must-have.* You earn that respect by demonstrating healthy leadership models. There will be a variety of leadership models available to you in the workplace, but far too many of them are pointing the way toward poor health, sleep deprivation, muddied priorities and weak decision-making. You have the power to embrace something different—to bring new hammers, and new nails to the table.

You'll need to take the time through a thoughtful leadership development process to identify what you stand for as a leader—and to capture that in writing. These types of *Leadership Credos* can serve as important anchors in times of storm, and through major transitions. They represent what we espouse as our personal values and principles, which manifest themselves in our leadership roles. In preparation for writing this book, I looked back at my own Leadership Credo, first written nearly a decade ago. I will be forever grateful to Greta Cowan, Leadership Coach, trusted colleague and one who I have the privilege of calling my friend, for taking that leg of my journey with me. Greta introduced me to this concept and coached me through the completion of this bedrock document. Today, the words and phrases contained in that document—*accountability, forthright communications, tough decision-making,* among many others—have even greater resonance with me than they did years ago. I've grown as a leader, and it pleases me to know that I'm still growing.

As you deepen your toolkit and set of experiences, both your value and the wealth of your options will increase. This is particularly useful should you experience an unexpected job loss. So, remember to fight hard to stay out of the boxes in which others may place you. Hold onto the belief that you are unique—as an individual, and as a professional in whatever field you've chosen.

Wherever you are on your journey, know that I'll be rooting for you.

Be forever #ToughAsNails!

Tough As Nails · Big Ideas

✓ Using your voice in the workplace will often mean facing resistance

✓ How and when you use your voice depends upon your company's culture, the level of support from the leadership ranks, and your own ambitions

✓ Resist the urge to speak until you have your facts straight

✓ Trade simply adding 'your two cents,' for opportunities to provide more substantive input

✓ Before speaking up, take the temperature (read the room, study body language)

✓ Develop the skill of precision when speaking—get rid of extraneous words and phrases

✓ Disagreement can spur better ideas. Disagreeing is a skill (pgs. 141-142)

✓ There are many antidotes to the *Impostor Syndrome* (pgs. 143-144)

✓ You are the ultimate owner of your career path

✓ Build a small, professional circle of colleagues in the field who can inspire you, speak words of wisdom, etc.

✓ Be the 'shiny penny' wherever you go (p. 146)

✓ Create a *Leadership Credo* to capture your personal leadership values and principles

Pearls from Jo's Journal

Who could have ever guessed that this shy girl from Brooklyn would be writing a book about finding one's voice?! What a journey! My mind goes back to being in an airport at about 9 or 10 years of age, waiting to board a plane to my parent's home country of Guyana. For reasons that I'm now too old to remember, we were waiting for hours. The entire travel experience felt endless. My older brother was practically bouncing off the walls and probably behaving as a perfectly normal young child...simply burning off the excess energy which was stored up from doing nothing. I, on the other hand, remained silent. When one of my aunts, who was traveling with us, commented on how well-behaved I was, I distinctly remember translating the words 'well-behaved' into 'perfect.' My lack of complaining and virtual silence during an otherwise chaotic scene, was considered perfection. So, there I was—dying to run, talk, and maybe even scream. Instead, I doubled-down on this perceived state of perfection and spent that part of the travel experience in silence. That made sense then. It seems ludicrous now. But, I'm glad I can remember it. I now count that moment as one of the many rungs on my life's ladder—where I've been climbing and climbing to this point where my voice is now used...a lot. These days, I not only use my voice to complain, however. I use it to advise, challenge, advocate, nurture, lead, and to love.

To the Men in our Lives

I love the men in my life—my husband, my sons, my brother, etc. They all bring their own authentically awesome selves to each encounter that I have with them. They are unafraid to think differently and they offer their own unique perspectives to every situation. I may not always agree with those perspectives, but I do value them.

For women to make the necessary strides in the workplace—and in every space—we need men. There have been many times when my husband offered a male point of view which opened my eyes to a completely different way of thinking about something.

The act itself of offering someone something different doesn't fully guarantee success, however. The offer must be made with respect and a sincere interest in the final outcome. And, the recipient must have the same, or greater degree of respect and interest in the outcome. That's the kind of balance needed in the workplace. A woman who is able to find—and use—her voice with power and influence in the workplace, will only be successful if others are willing to listen to what she is communicating.

As for the male/female dynamic, it should *never* be a zero-sum game. I'm disappointed when I see a woman turn it into one. A woman's gain must never mean a man's loss. We need each other. Inclusivity can only occur if we're all committed to a melting pot of ideas and perspectives whose source becomes irrelevant.

When I think of this on a larger scale, my mind goes to 2017—the year of #MeToo. My deepest desire is that the ensuing years would come to reflect an #UsToo mentality—where men and women are working hand-in-hand on our most plaguing issues. Debjani Biswas, Speaker, Author of #UsToo: Bridging the Gender Gap, and self-proclaimed 'Exclusion Exterminator,' captures this concept most brilliantly in her September 15, 2018 LinkedIn article entitled *No *B.R.I.D.G.E. too far. Can you 'listen as if you might be wrong?'* Biswas shares her vision "*that decent and strong women AND men would work together* to bridge the global gender gap." She goes on further to state what I believe to be a sobering truth: "If we continue to stay within our corners and blame not just the other individual, but the group that individual comes from—we will move further behind. We cannot afford to widen the gender gap. #UsToo—Together—Matters. We must bridge this chasm—one interaction at a time."

To all of my wonderful brothers: *thank you* for helping all of the women in your lives to show up in today's workplace with their most authentic and powerful voices.

---

*(**B**uilding and **R**einforcing **I**nclusion can only occur after we have **D**estroyed the **G**uardrails of **E**xclusion)—*Debjani Biswas*

Notes

Chapter 1:
Your Special Sauce

1. Center for American Progress: The Women's Leadership Gap, Women's Leadership by the Numbers 21 May 2017

2. VIA is scientifically validated by Robert McGrath, Ph.D. and provides a rank order of an adult's 24-character strengths

3. The foundation for the DISC model comes from the work of a Harvard psychologist named Dr. William Moulton Marston in the 1920's

4. Eva Pomerantz, Ellen Alterman, and Jill Saxon (2002, p. 402)

5. Indiana University. "Men Do Hear--But Differently Than Women, Brain Images Show." ScienceDaily. ScienceDaily, 29 November 2000.

Chapter 2:
Be the Sharpest Nail in Your Company's Chest

6. Business Insider: 9 places in the US where job candidates may never have to answer the dreaded salary question again 10 April 201

   https://www.businessinsider.com/places-where-salary-question-banned-us-2017-10

Chapter 3:
Unblock Your Own Path to Being *Authentically Awesome*

7. Pew Research Study November 12-21, 2014 N=1,835

8. The Gulf of Mexico oil spill occurred on April 20, 2010 on the Deepwater Horizon oil rig. It was the worst marine oil spill in the history of the petroleum industry

9. Pew Research Study (above) found that, among those who drew a distinction on the trait of decisiveness, 27% of adults surveyed believed that men are more decisive than women; only 9% believed the opposite

Chapter 4:
Drop the Hammer on that Mean-Girl Culture!

10. Gallup: US Engagement Survey as of August 2017

Chapter 7:
You May Bend, But You Won't Break

11. US Department of Labor: Bureau of Labor Statistics Economic News Release September 2016

Chapter 8:
Race and Age Factors

12. *Over 40 and Interviewing? Have these things happened to you?* Jo Weech, LinkedIn Article July 2018

Chapter 9:
Reinventing Yourself

13. The Potential of Cognitive Neuroscience for Information Systems Research. Dimoka, Pavlou, Davis 14 April 2010

Chapter 10:
Embrace the BOSS in You!

14. The Impostor Phenomenon: Recent Research Findings Regarding Dynamics, Personality and Family Patterns and Their Implications for Treatment. Langord, Clance. Volume 30/Fall 1993/Number 3

Index

Made in the
USA
Middletown, DE